Phenom:

THE EXCELLENCE OF EXECUTION

Dr. Greg Jackson

Inner3 Productions

Phenom by Greg Jackson

Printed by CreateSpace

ISBN: 1450542921

9781450542920

Contents

About the Composer

Greg Jackson is an active performer, clinician and educator across the nation. He received the Bachelor of Science degree in Music Composition/Theory from Austin Peay State University, the Master of Music degree in Music Theory/Composition from The University of Alabama, and the Doctor of Musical Arts degree in Percussion Performance at the University of Alabama. While in Tuscaloosa during his residence at UA, Jackson was a percussion assistant for the Million Dollar Band drum line in 2000, 2002, and 2005 as well as various ensembles in the Southeast region. Dr. Jackson marched snare drum with Eklipse Percussion Ensemble in 1999 and was on the staff in 2001 with the WGI independent open champions. At the Percussive Arts Society International Collegiate Snare Competition he placed in the top 10 four consecutive years and top 4 two years. He has also been associated as a consultant with three Drum Corps International Individuals champions and 1 PASIC Individuals champion. Jackson has performed with numerous artists including Nancy Zeltsman, Michael Burritt, Tomas Cruz, and Bob Mintzer of the Yellow Jackets. Dr. Jackson is endorsed by Remo Inc., Pearl Percussion and Pro-mark sticks and mallets. He is the author of the book *The Synergy Method for Drumming* and will soon release a DVD titled *Elements of Synergy*.

ACKNOWLEDGMENTS

I would like to take this time to thank all those who have believed in me and encouraged me all of these times. First, I must acknowledge all that Jesus Christ has done for me. Without Him I would not have the vision or the strength to write and perform any of the music I am able to share with the world.

Thank you to my lovely wife Autumn. You are truly amazing, patient and understanding. You continue to encourage me and keep the drive going while I pursue my dreams. Thankfully my biggest dream came true when I met you.

Thank you to all of my family and friends, especially those I was not able to mention in the first book. You know who you are! I don't say this enough, but you are all extremely important to me.

Thank you to Chris Hart at Remo, Inc., Staci Stokes and Kelly Strait at Pro-Mark, and Joe Fant at Pearl for the continued support.

Thank you to my first composition teacher Dr. Jeff Wood for teaching me all that I know about composition. You continue to be a great mentor and friend.

This work is dedicated to my mom and the memory of my dad for putting up with the constant practice at all hours of the night and paying for all of my first lessons. You all helped me to become the disciplined and dedicated man that I am today.

And thank you to all that play the music I write. I feel honored that I am able to share the passion of drumming with you all. Always feel free to contact me for help because I think that is what the percussion community is all about, helping others achieve their goals.

All The Best,

G. Jackson

Legend

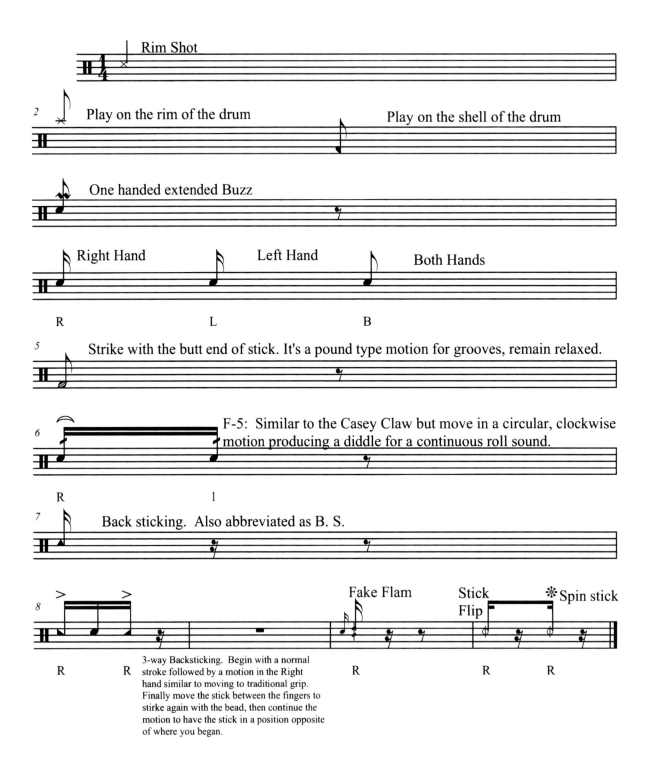

Rim Shot

Play on the rim of the drum

Play on the shell of the drum

One handed extended Buzz

Right Hand   Left Hand   Both Hands

R   L   B

Strike with the butt end of stick. It's a pound type motion for grooves, remain relaxed.

F-5: Similar to the Casey Claw but move in a circular, clockwise motion producing a diddle for a continuous roll sound.

R   l

Back sticking. Also abbreviated as B. S.

Fake Flam   Stick Flip   ✳ Spin stick

R   R

3-way Backsticking. Begin with a normal stroke followed by a motion in the Right hand similar to moving to traditional grip. Finally move the stick between the fingers to stirke again with the bead, then continue the motion to have the stick in a position opposite of where you began.

R   R   R

Resolution

Moderato ♩ = c. 109

G. Jackson

Resolution

Resolution

Resolution

Resonate

G. Jackson

10

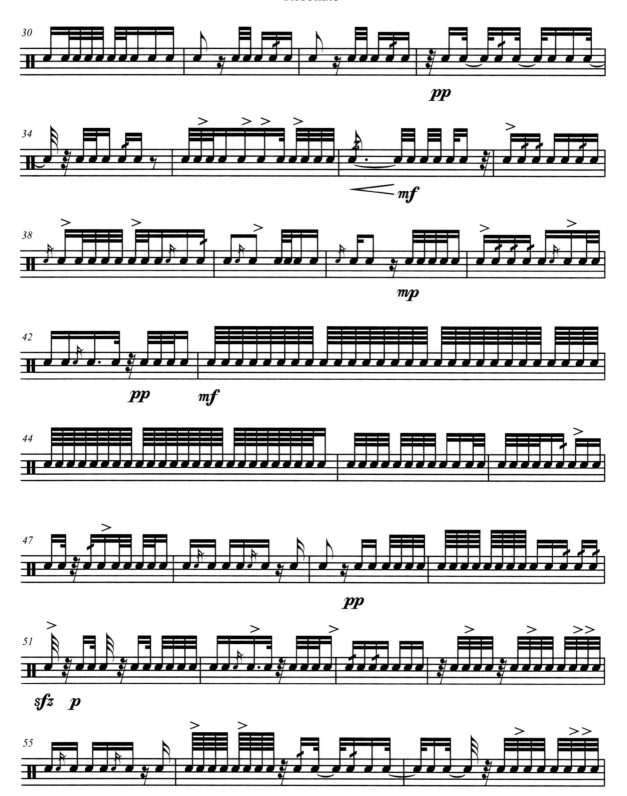

Resonate

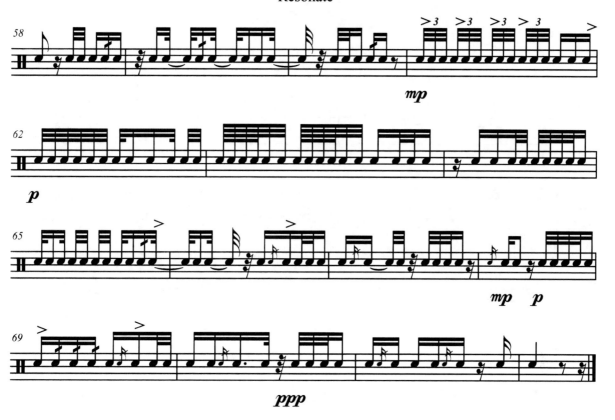

Risk, Que?

G. Jackson

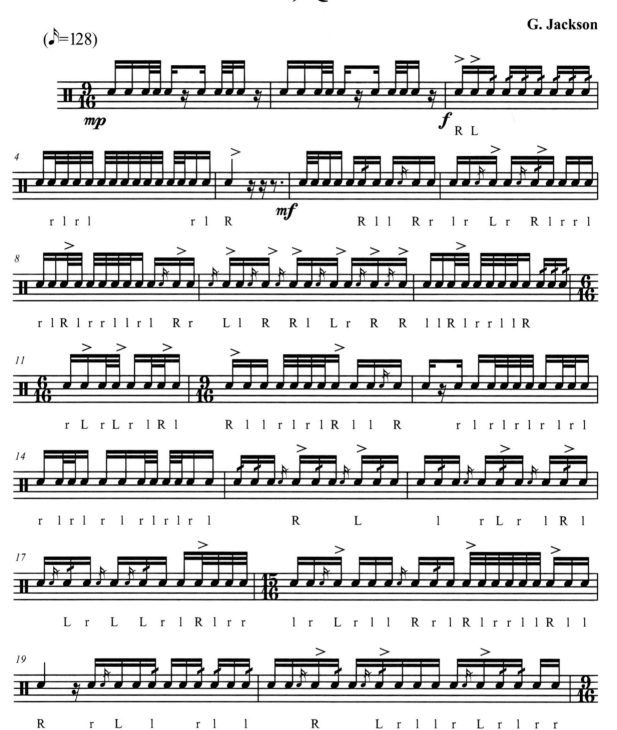

Risk, Que?

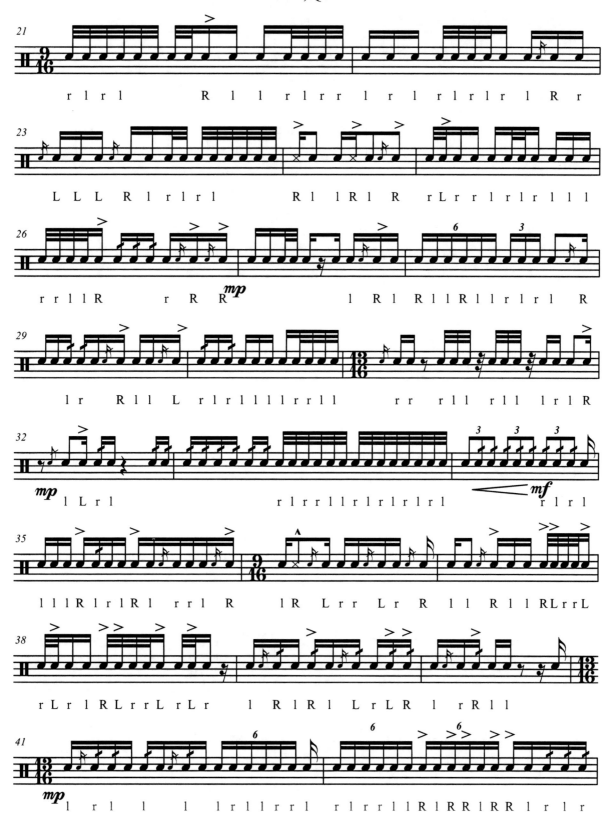

14

Risk, Que?

15

Risk, Que?

Shock Value

G. Jackson

18

Shock Value

19

Shock Value

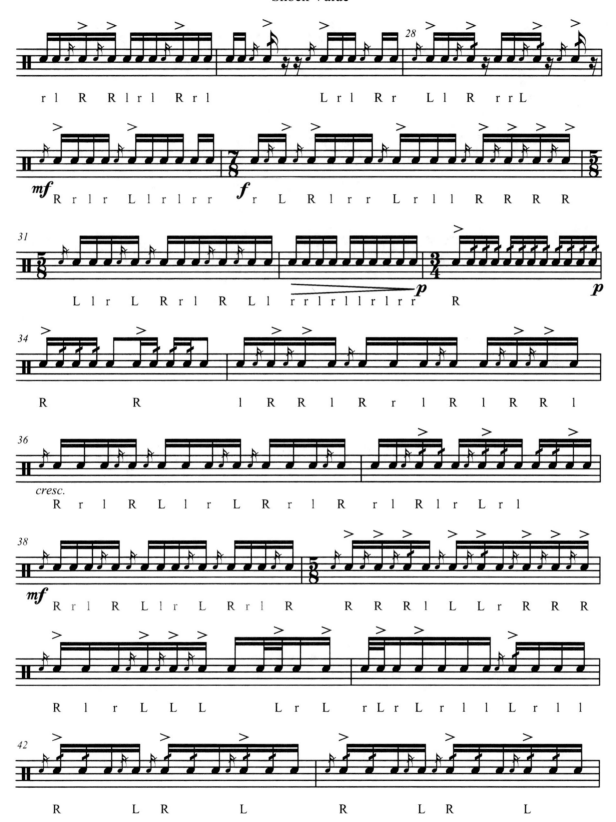

20

Shock Value

Skism

G. Jackson

Skism

23

Skism

24

Skism

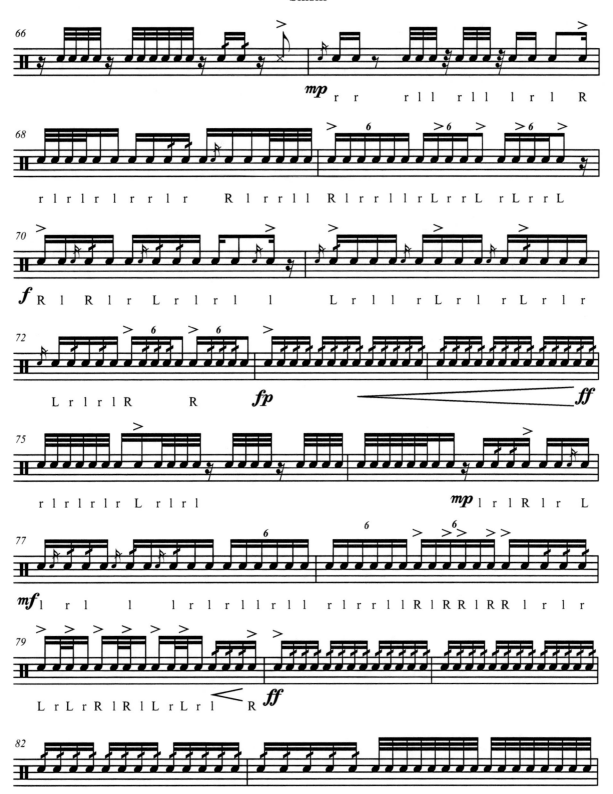

26

Skism

Sugar and Spice

G. Jackson

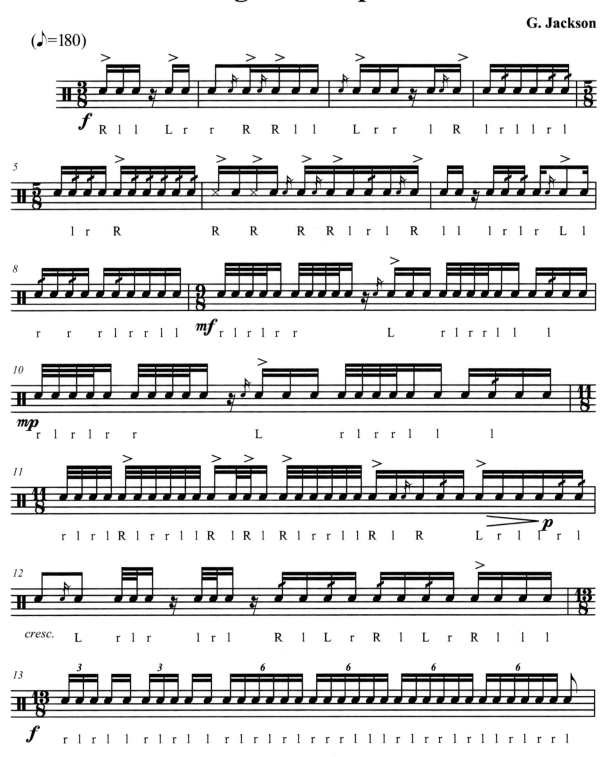

Sugar and Spice

29

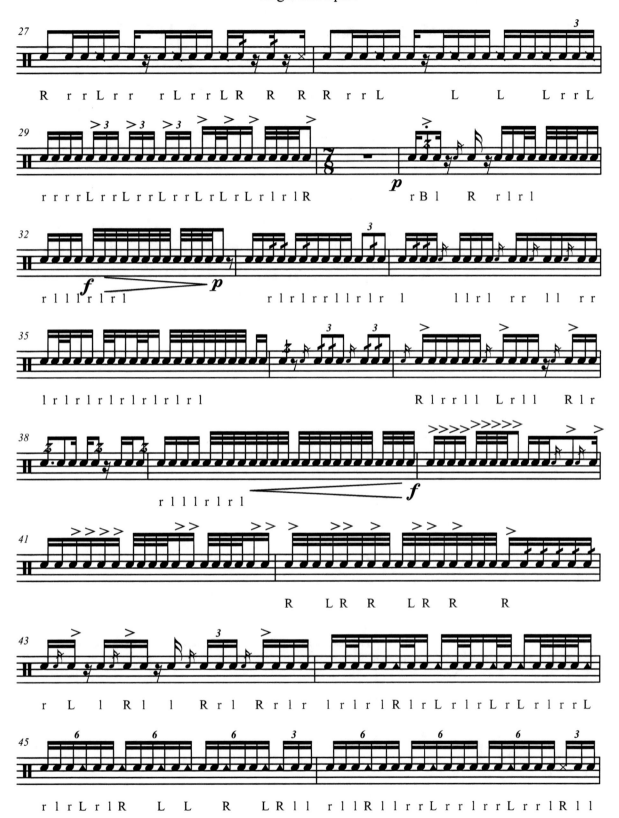

Sugar and Spice

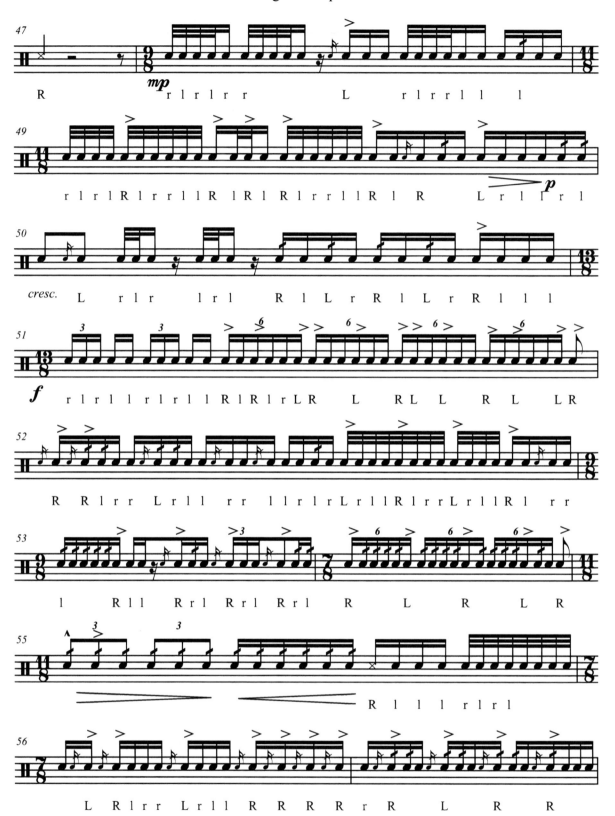

Sugar and Spice

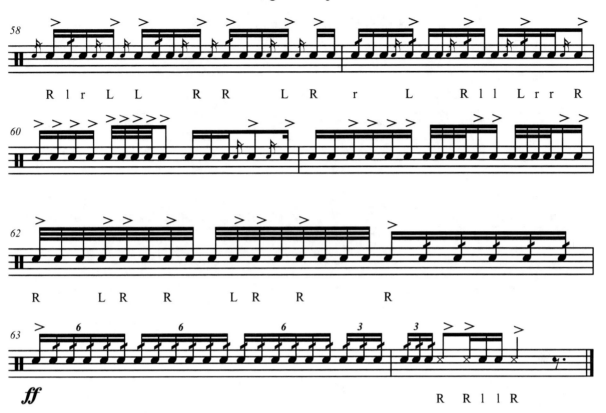

32

Sweet Aggression

G. Jackson

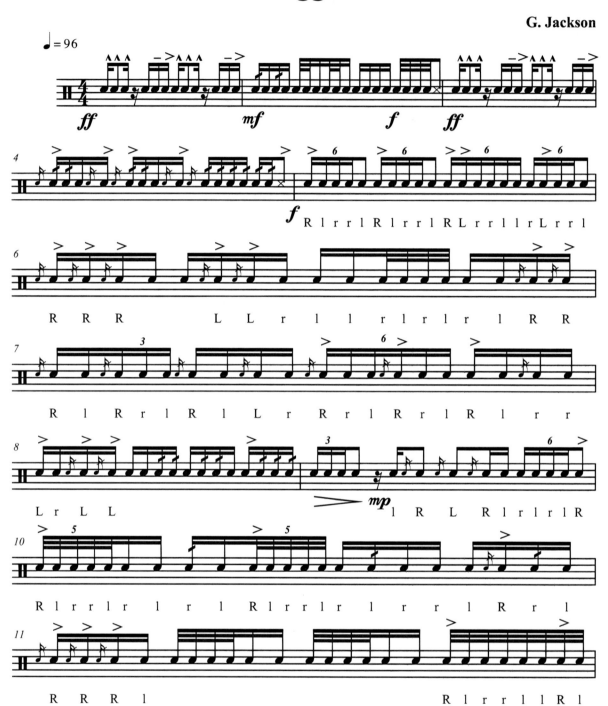

33

Sweet Aggression

34

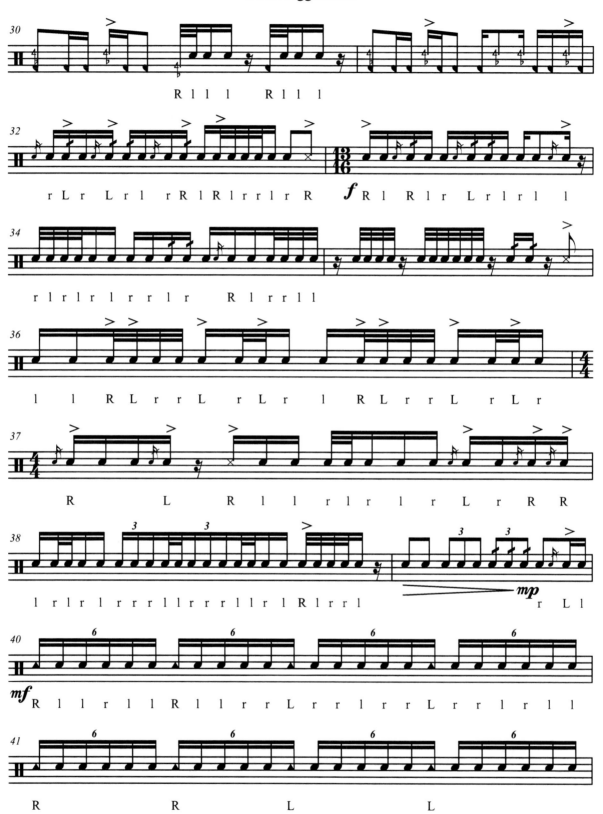

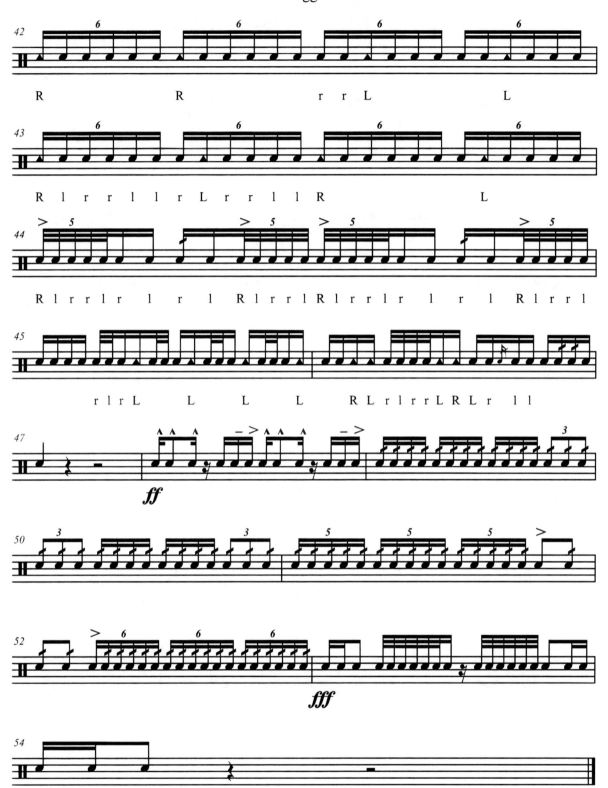

The Brain Trust Theory

G. Jackson

Moderato

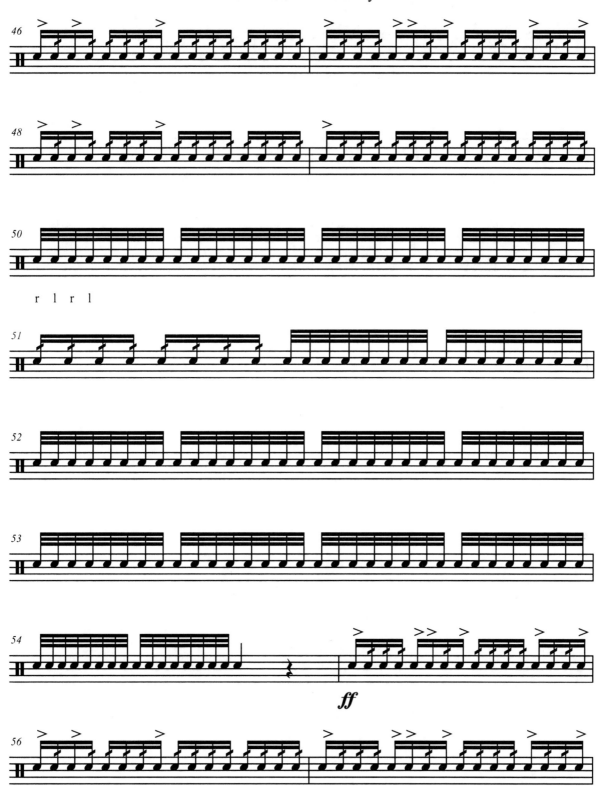

The Brain Trust Theory

41

Untouchable

G. Jackson

Pesante, Med-Fast

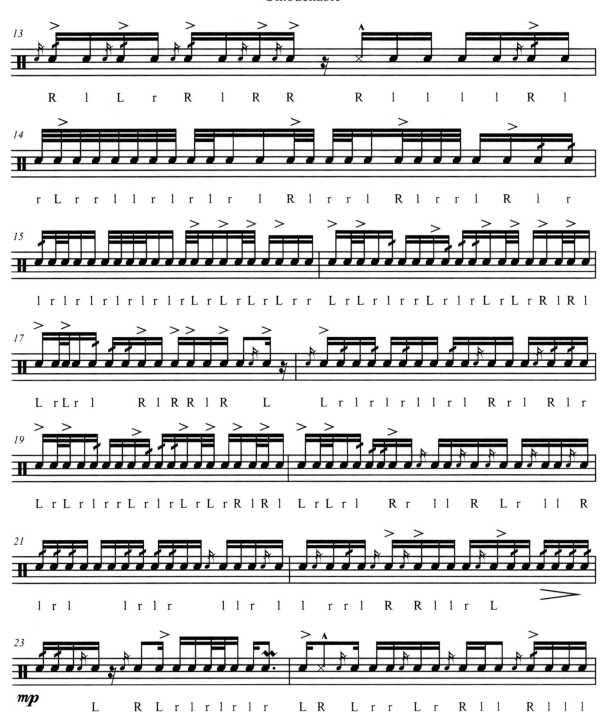

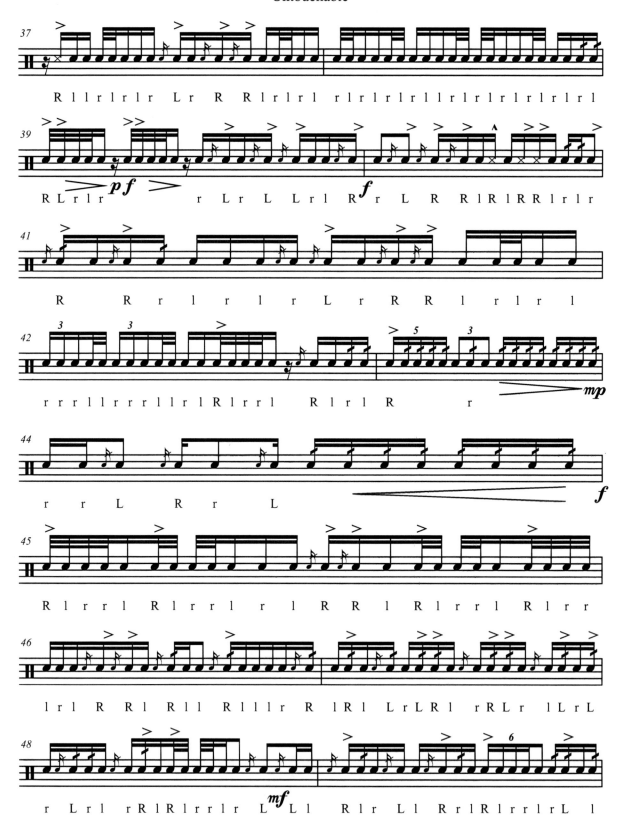

Untouchable

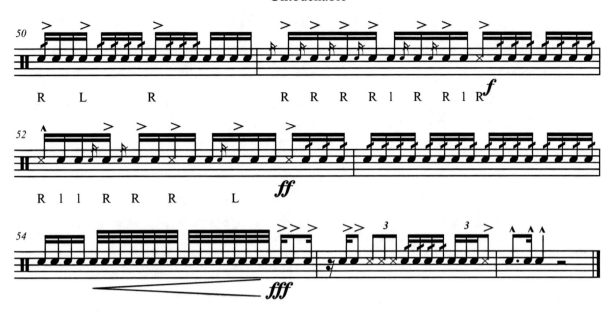

Zero Gravity

G. Jackson

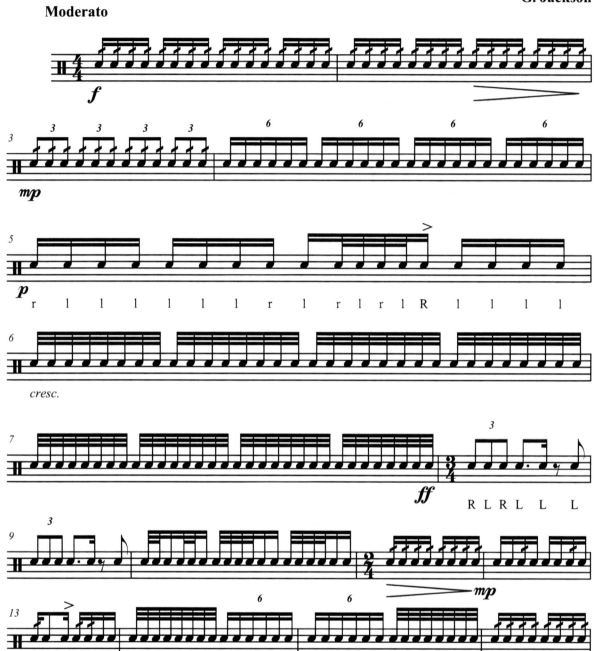

Zero Gravity

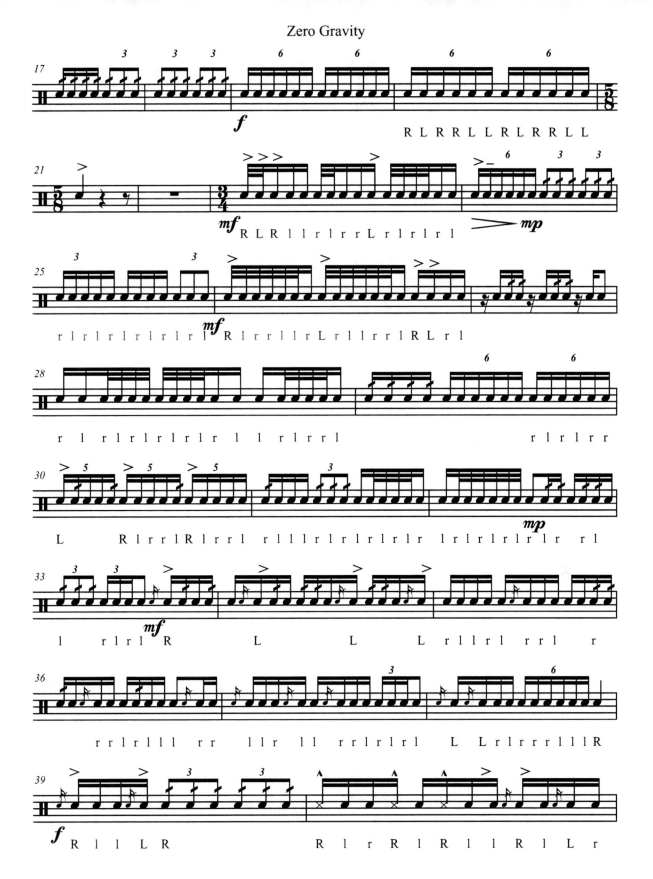

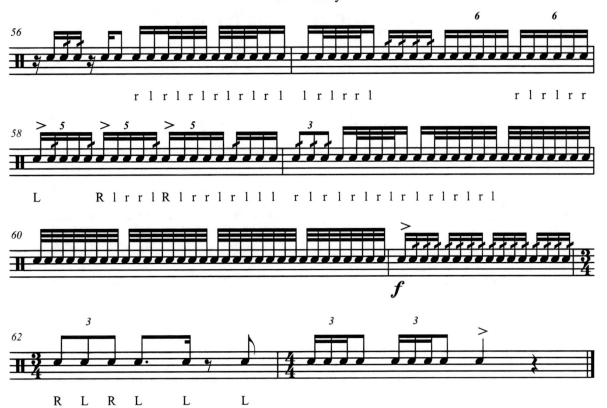

Balance of Harmony

G. Jackson

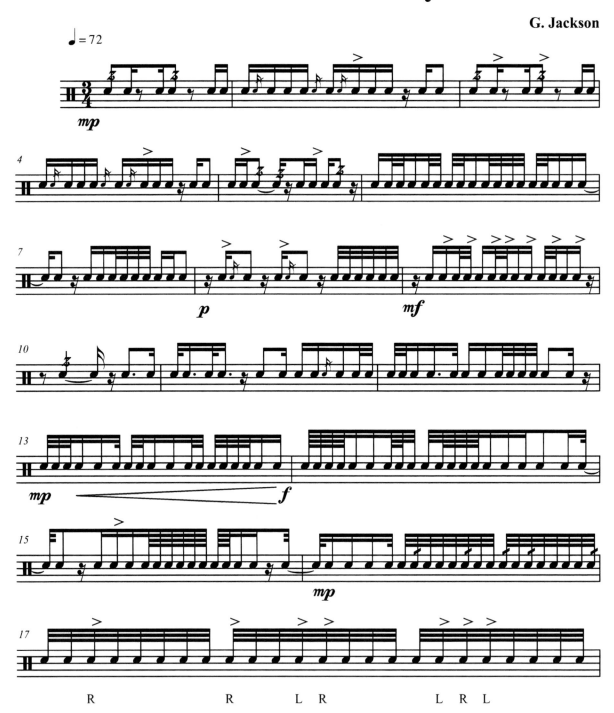

51

Balance of Harmony

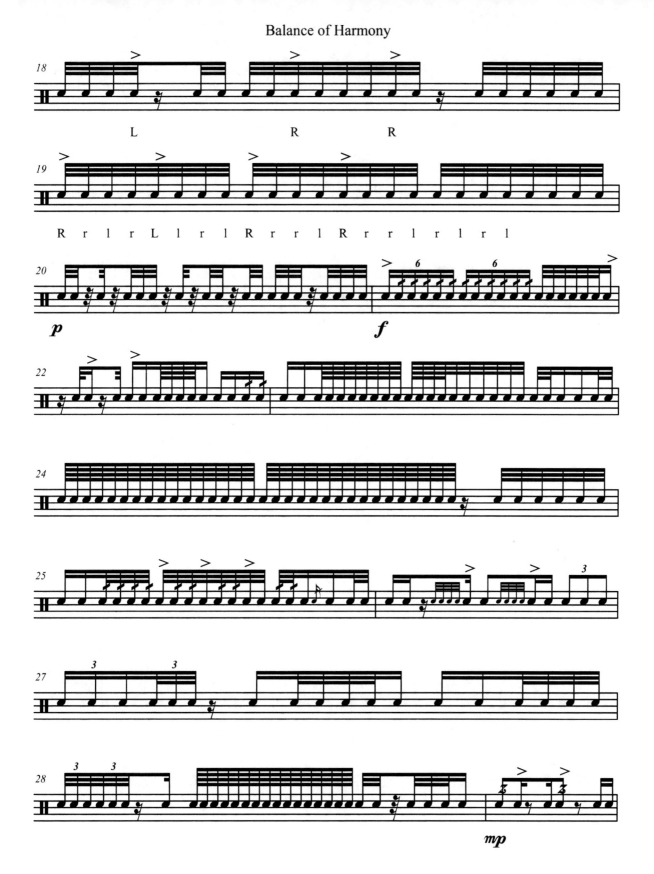

52

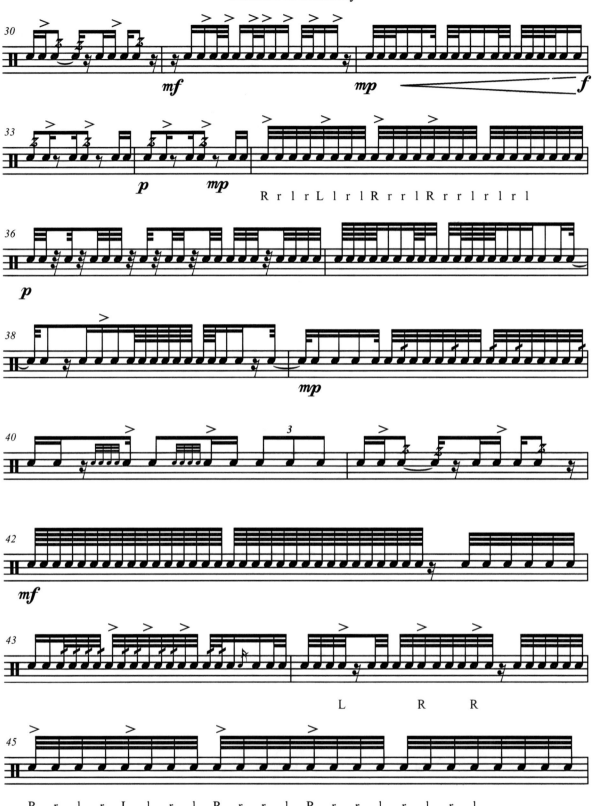

Balance of Harmony

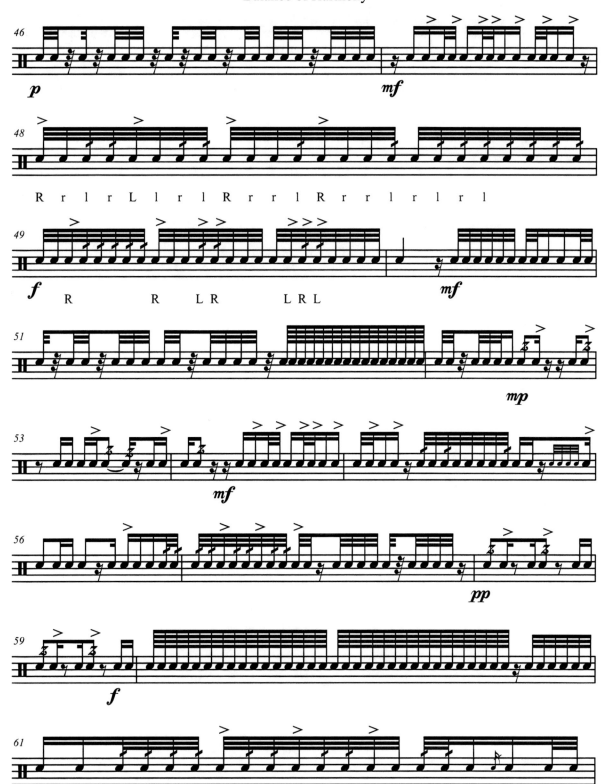

54

Balance of Harmony

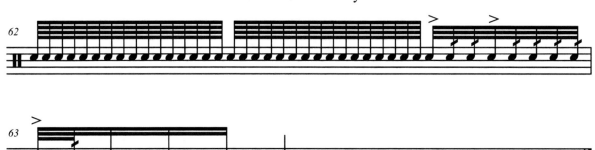

Bethseda (House of Mercy)

G. Jackson

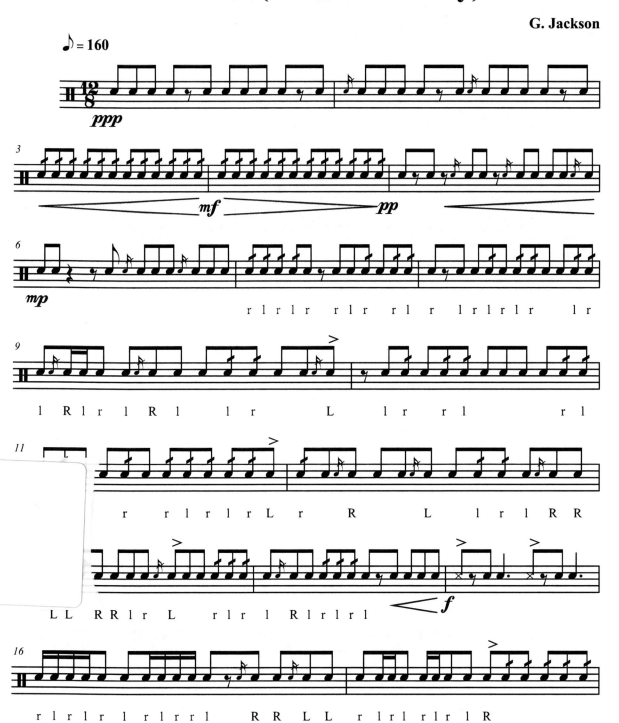

Bethseda (House of Mercy)

57

Broken Walls

G. Jackson

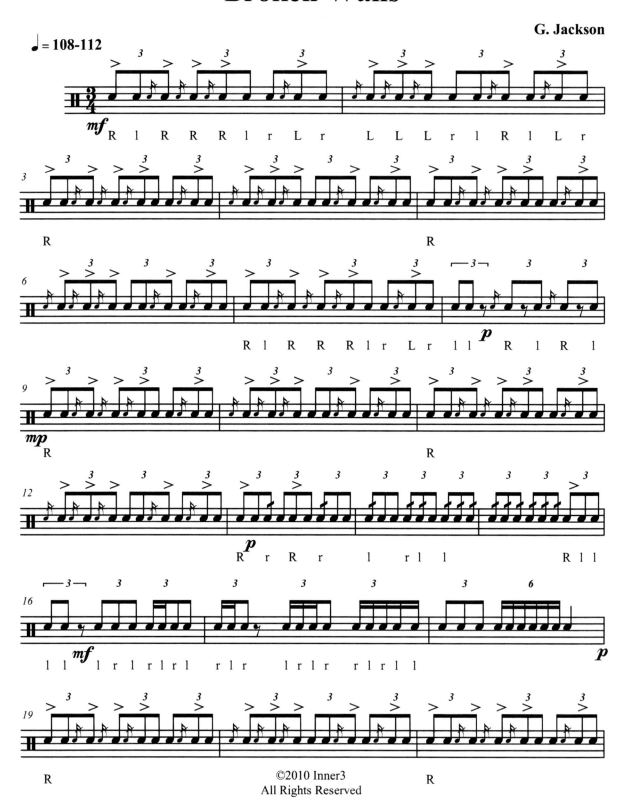

Broken Walls

Broken Walls

61

Broken Walls

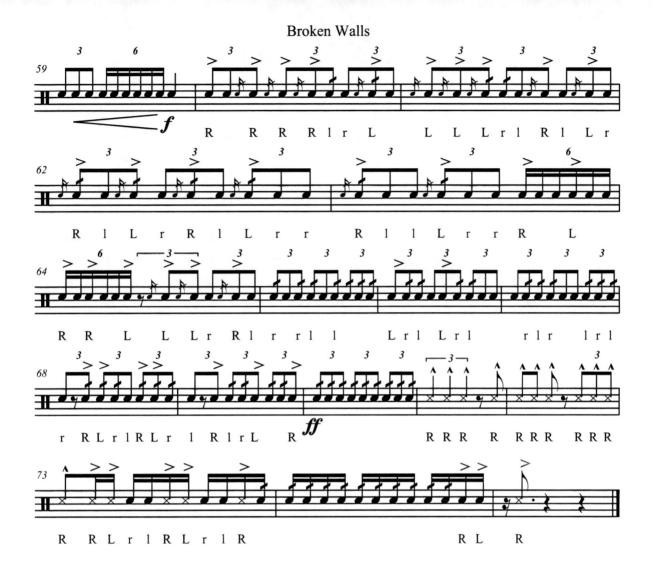

62

Cold Blooded

G. Jackson

Fast Groove

Cold Blooded

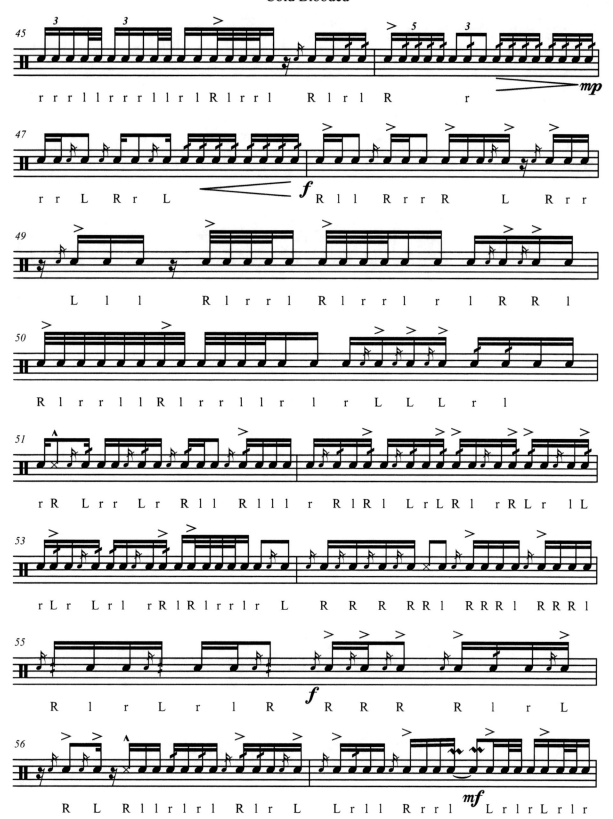

Cold Blooded

67

Cut Like a Sling Blade

G. Jackson

Cut Like a Sling Blade

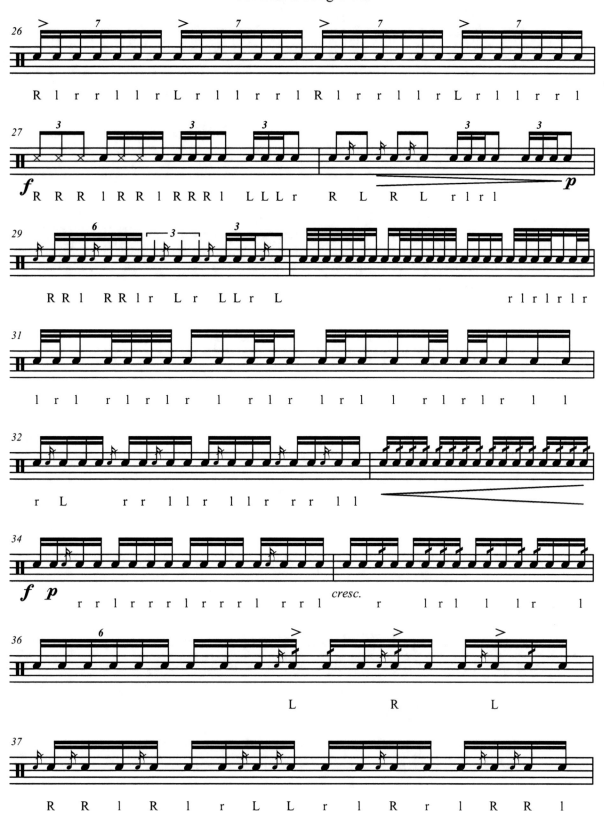

70

Cut Like a Sling Blade

71

Cut Like a Sling Blade

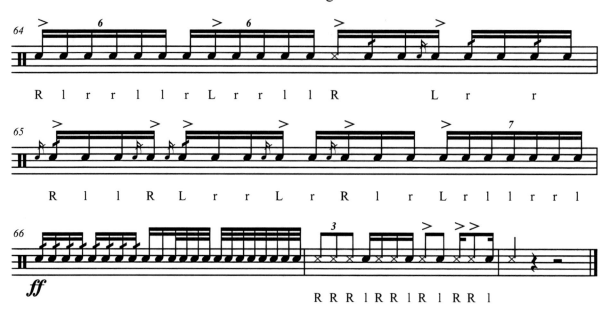

ff

R R R l R R l R l R R l

73

Dark to Light

G. Jackson

Dark to Light

75

Declaration of Faith

G. Jackson

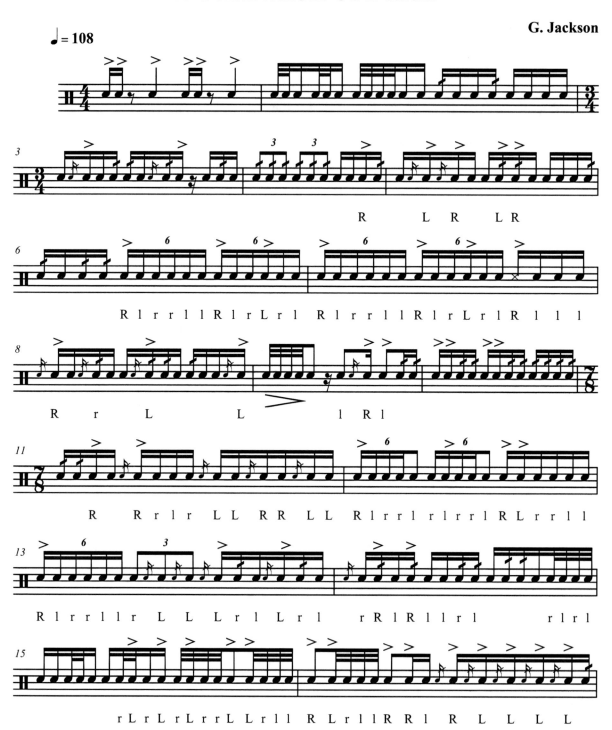

Declaration of Faith

79

Declaration of Faith

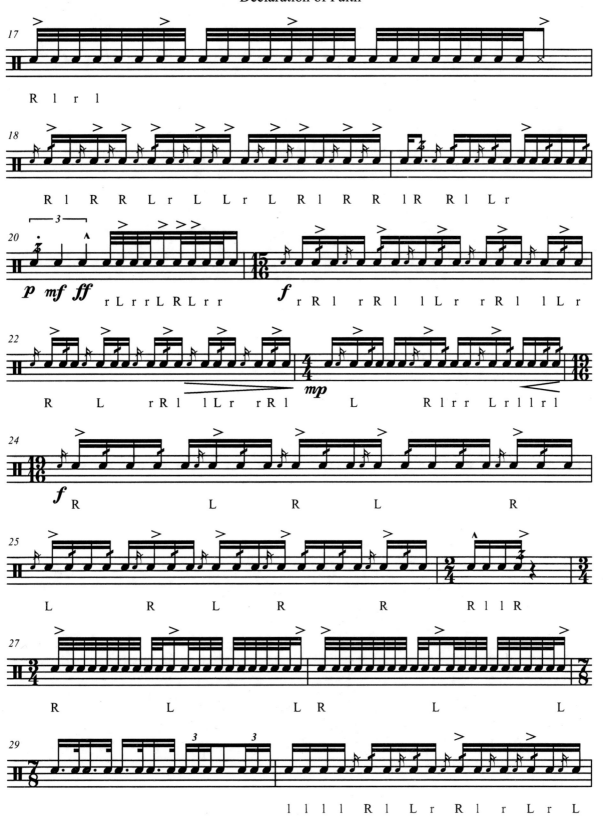

78

Declaration of Faith

79

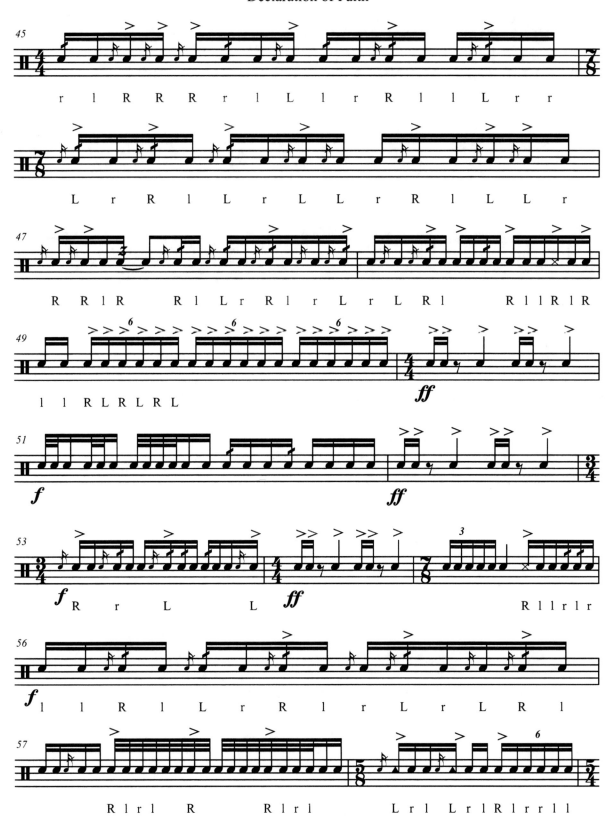

Declaration of Faith

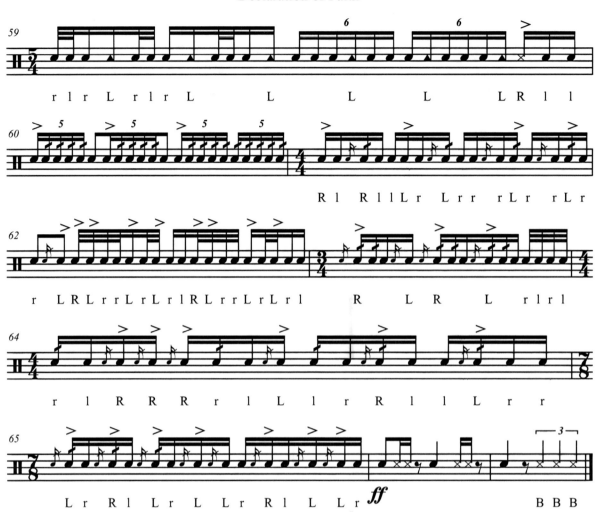

81

Defending Ghosts

G. Jackson

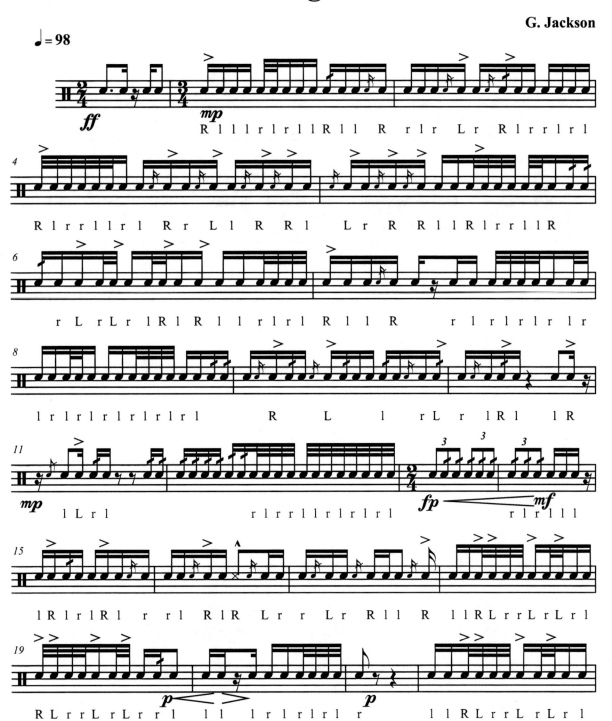

82

Defending Ghosts

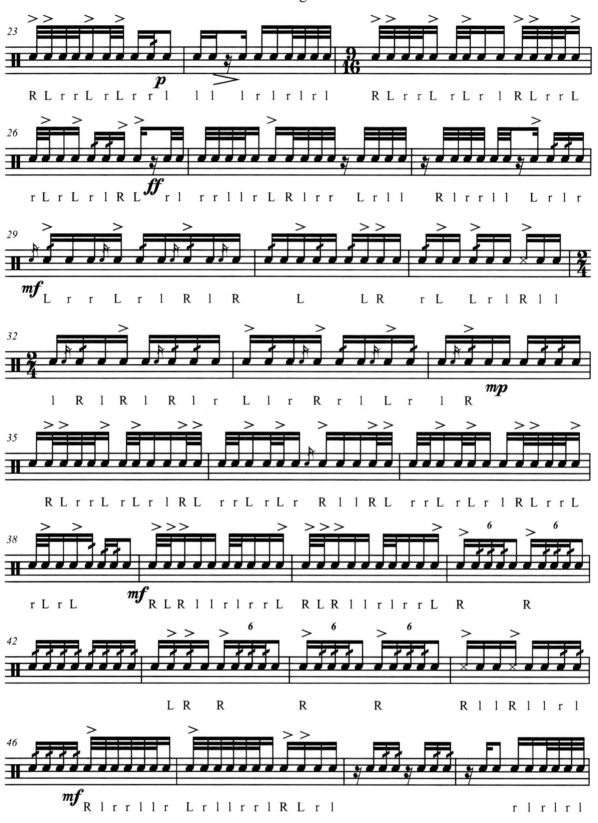

83

Defending Ghosts

Flow

G. Jackson

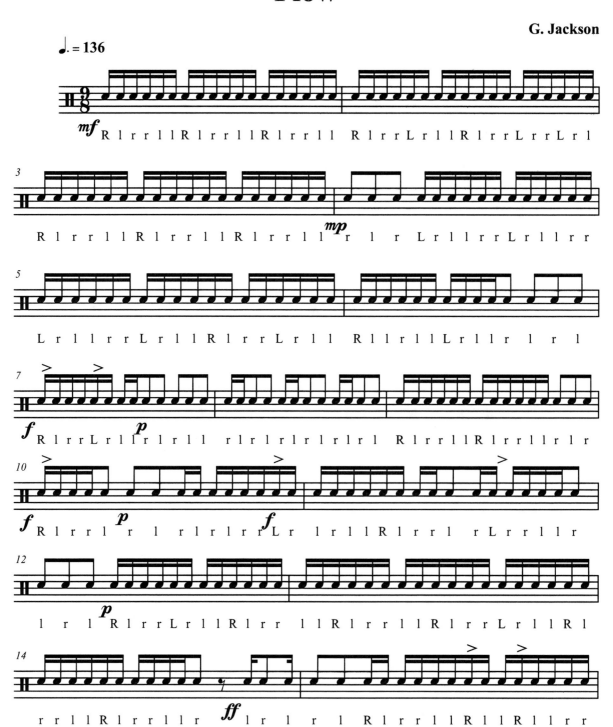

Flow

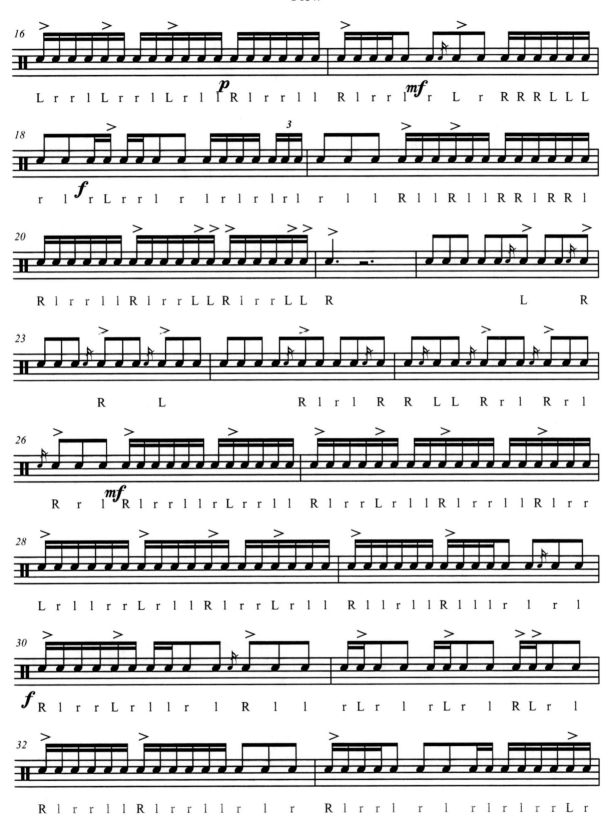

86

Flow

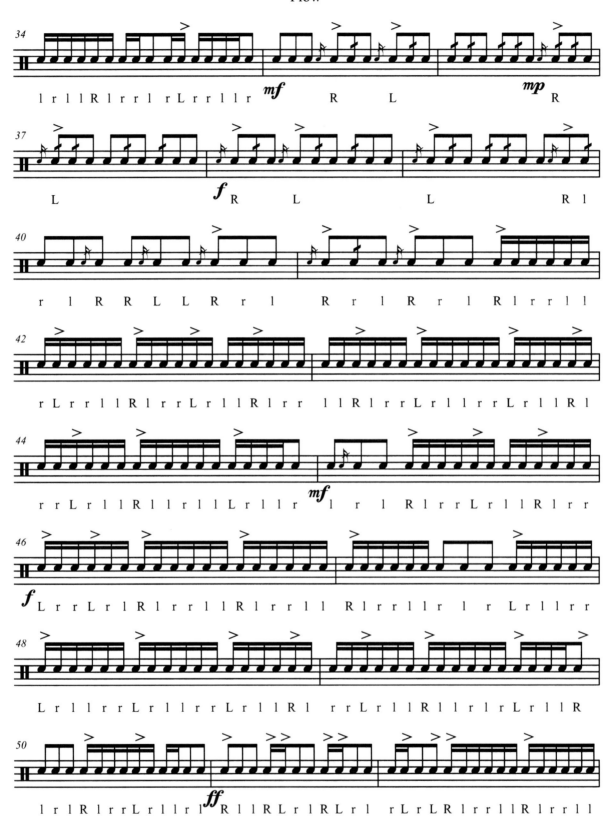

Flow

High Definition

G. Jackson

Groove

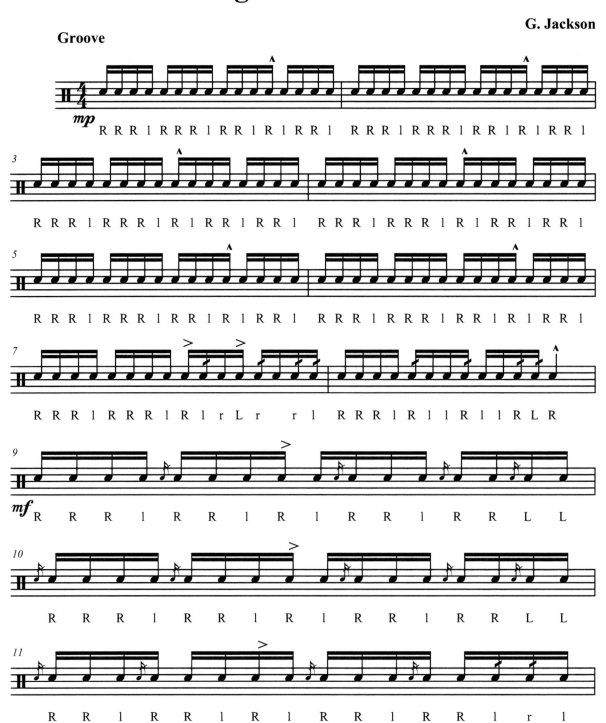

High Definition

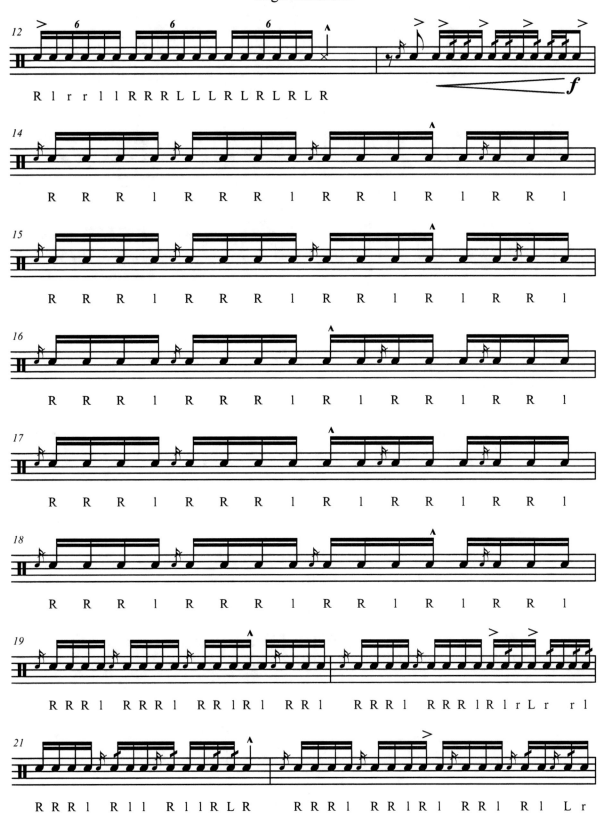

High Definition

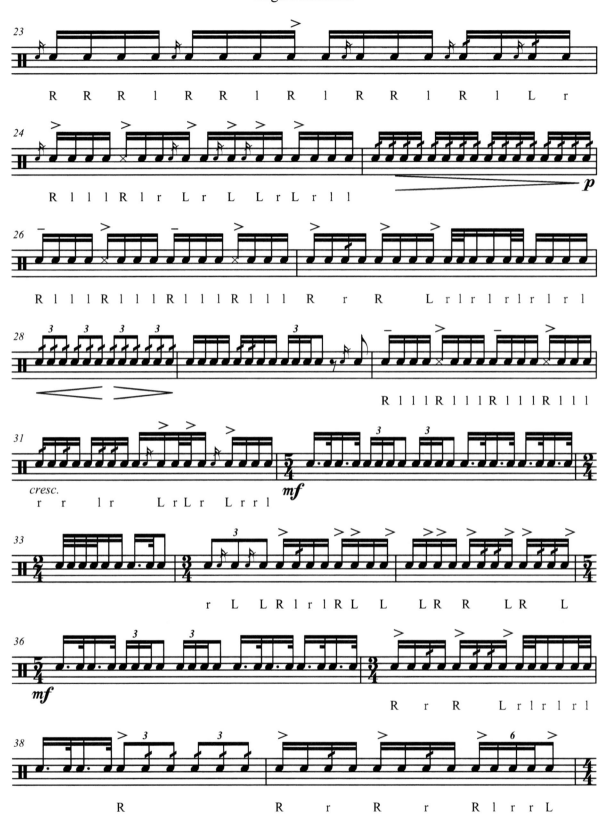

High Definition

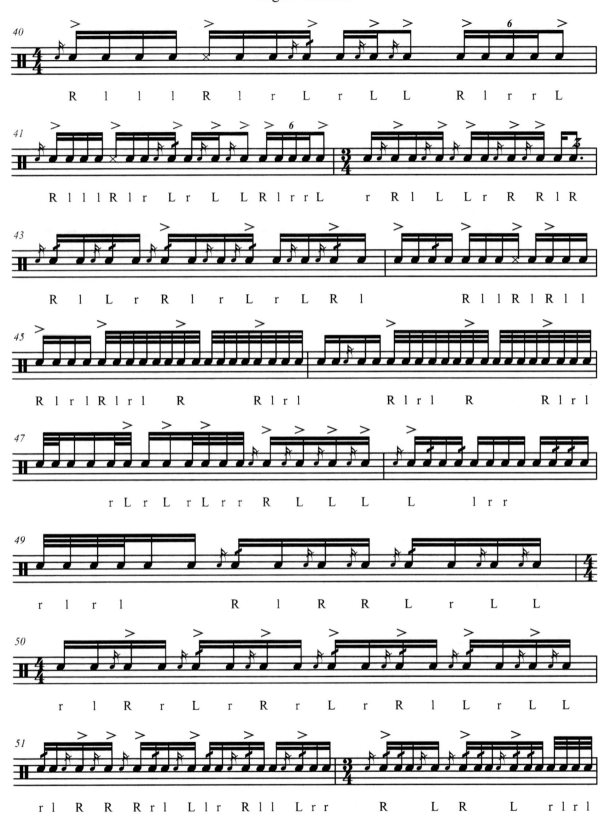

92

High Definition

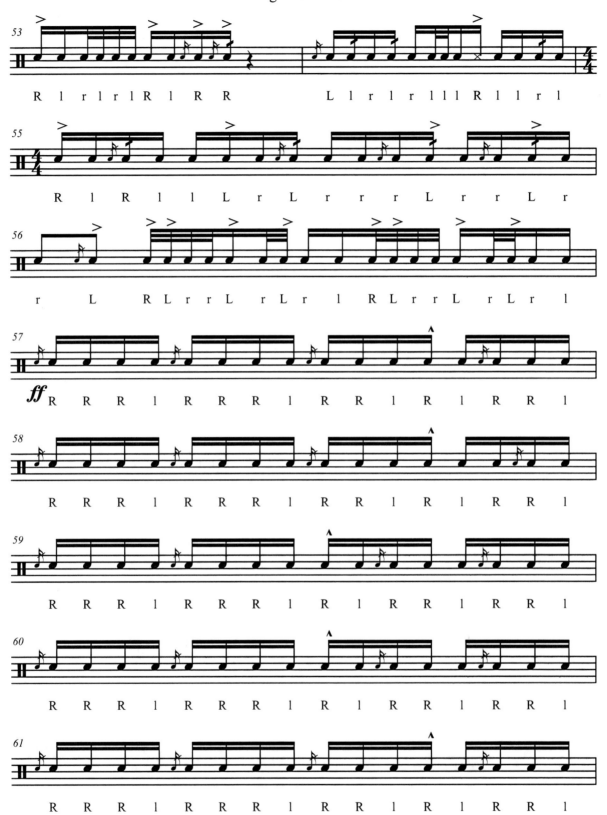

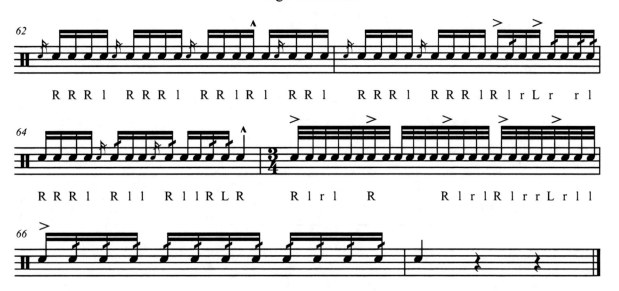

I Need Some Heat!

G. Jackson

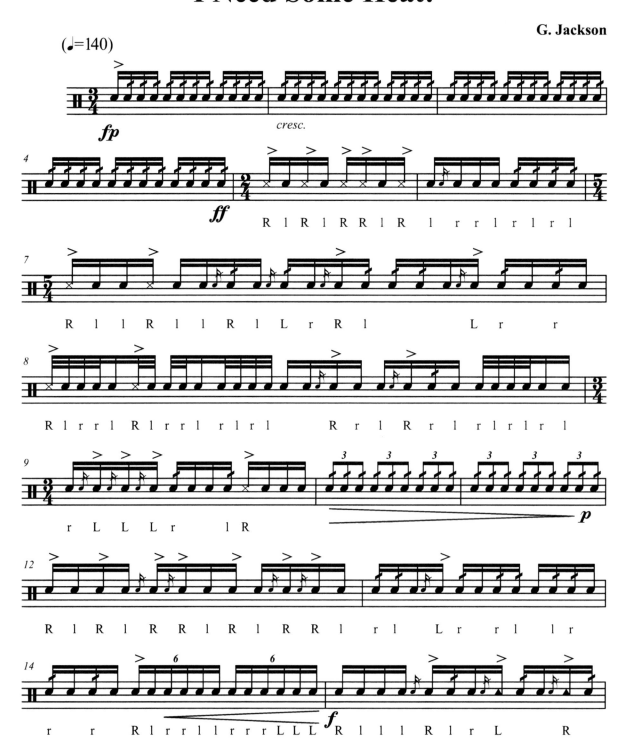

I Need Some Heat!

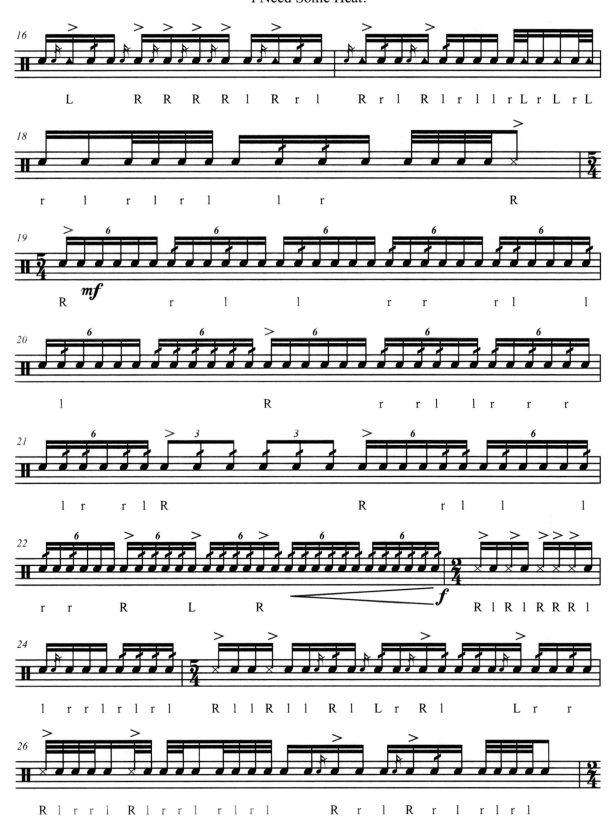

96

I Need Some Heat!

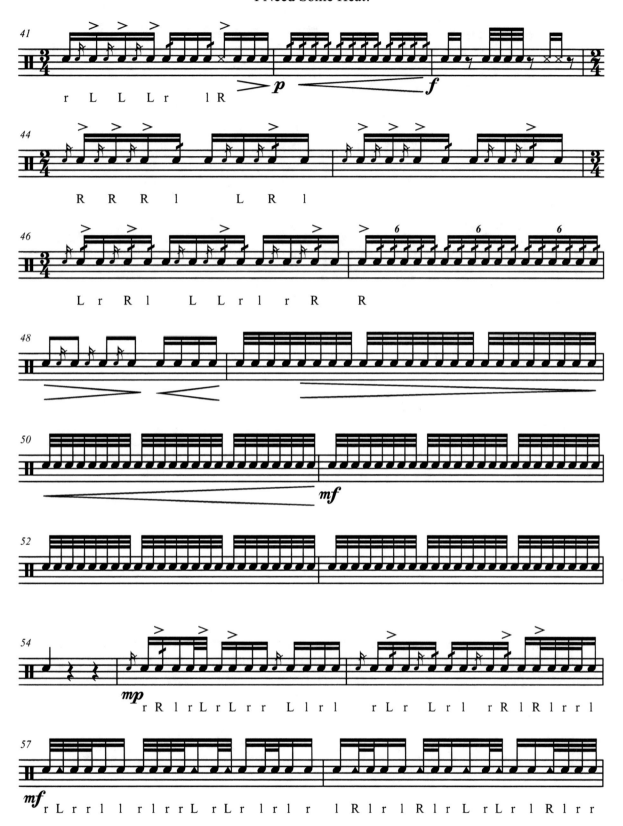

I Need Some Heat!

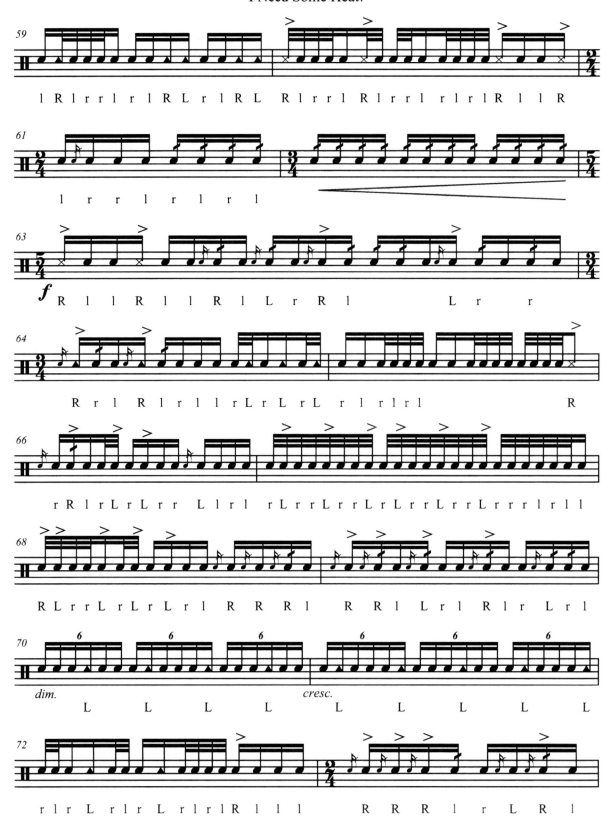

99

I Need Some Heat!

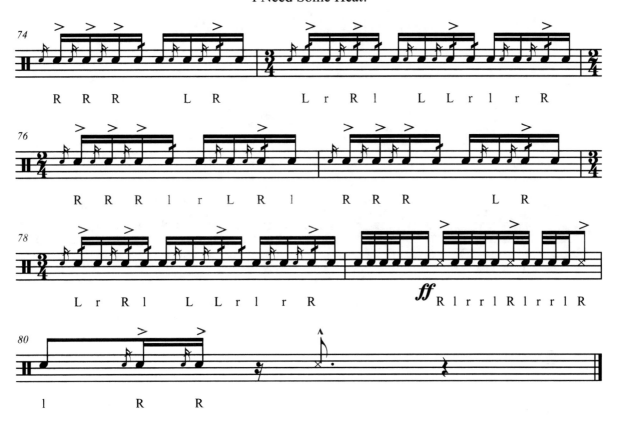

Illusions of Grandeur

G. Jackson

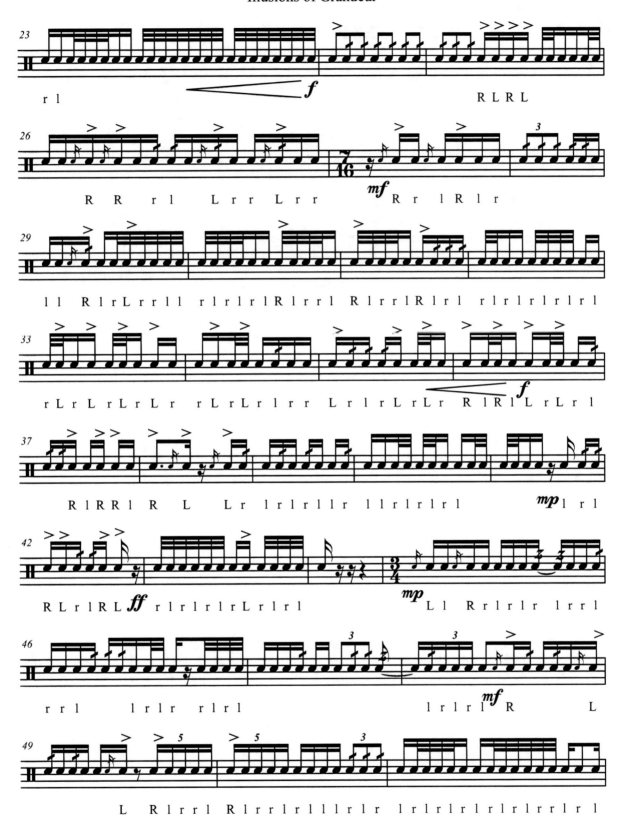

Let it be Written

G. Jackson

Let it be Written

Let it be Written

Let it be Written

Nostalgia

G. Jackson

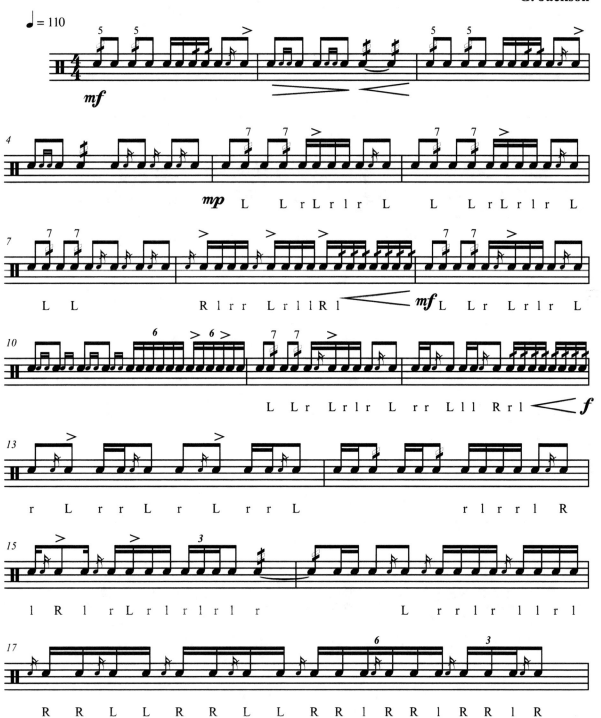

Nostalgia

109

Nostalgia

110

Nostalgia

111

Out of the Shadows

G. Jackson

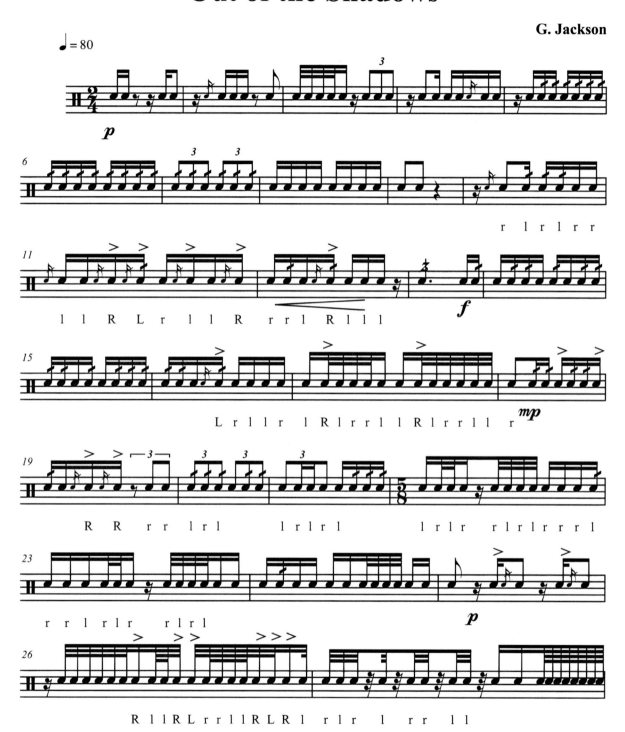

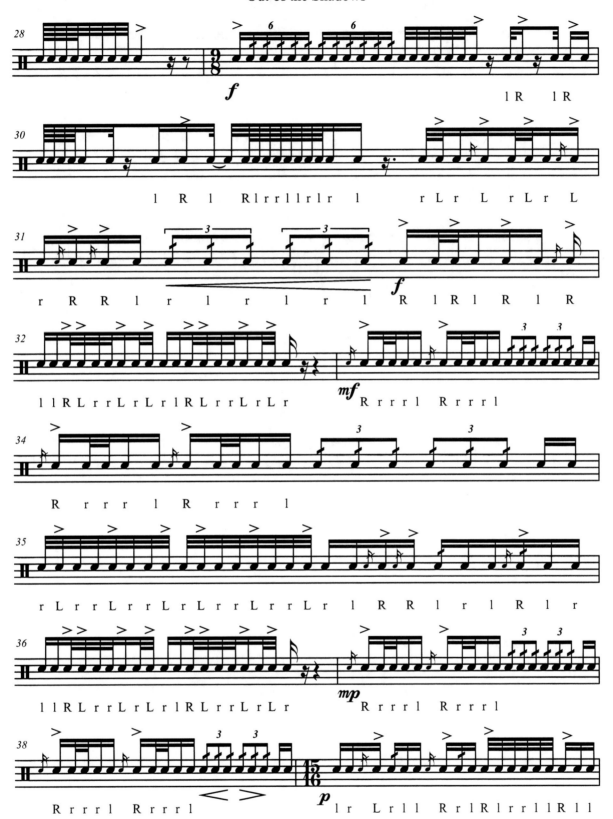

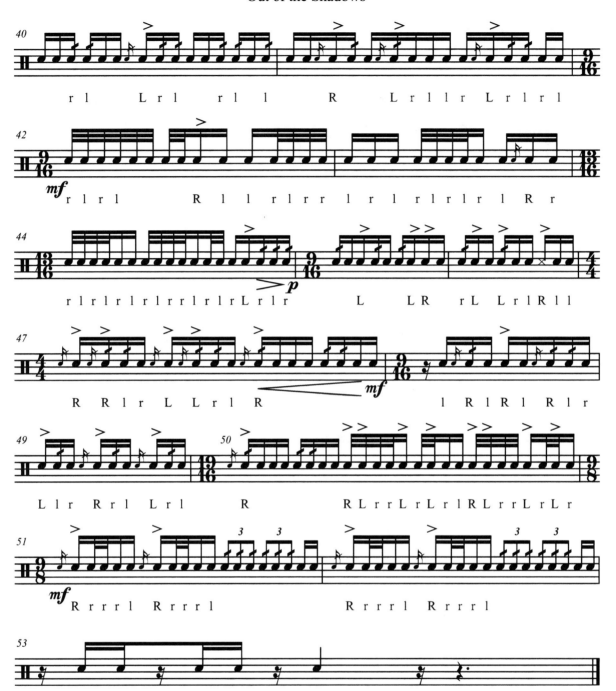

Overdrive

G. Jackson

116

Overdrive

118

Overdrive

119

Overdrive

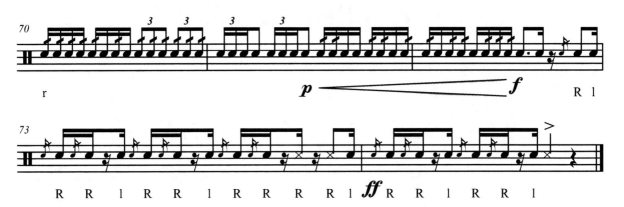

Perception is Reality

G. Jackson

Allegro

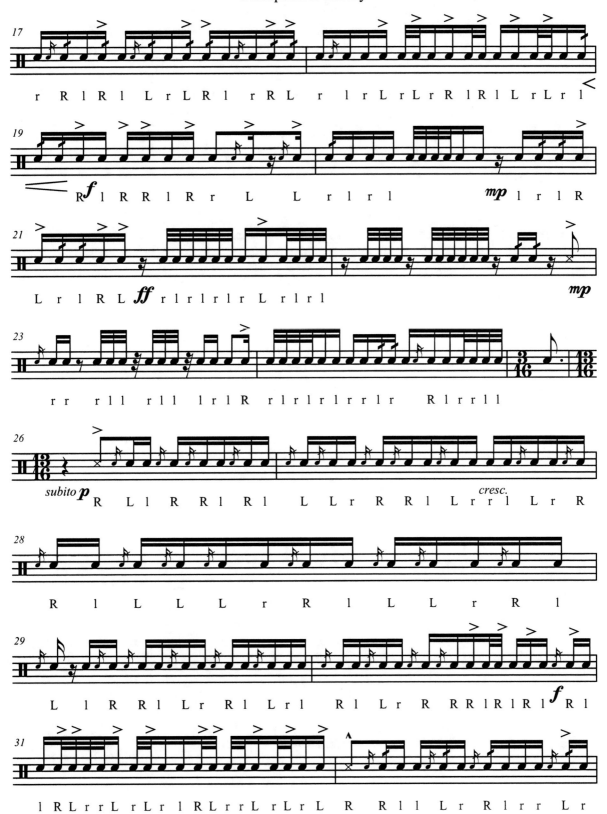

Perception is Reality

Eye of the Storm
PASIC 2003

G. Jackson

126

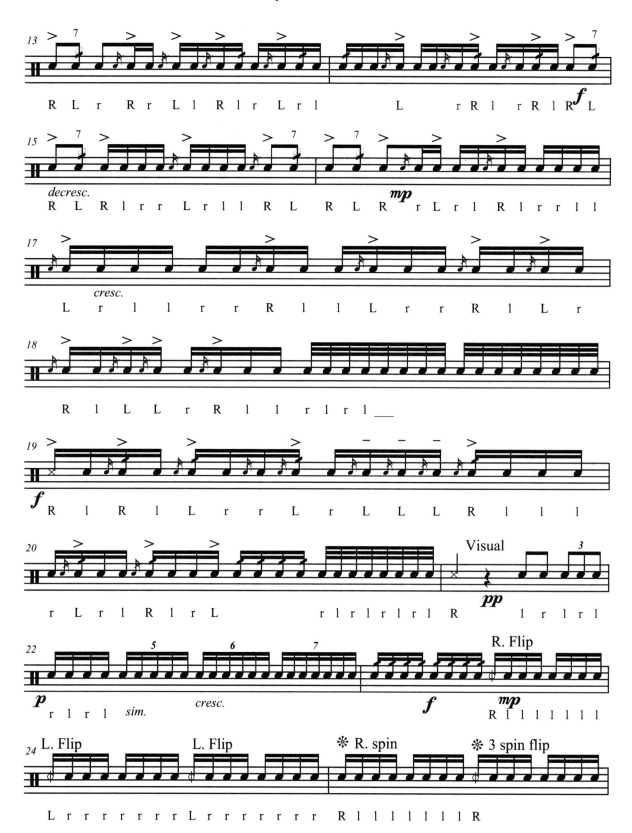

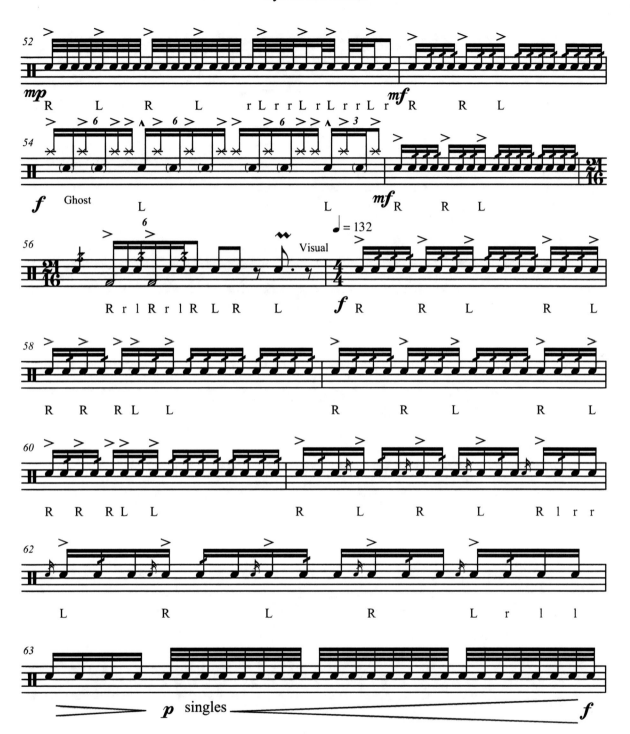

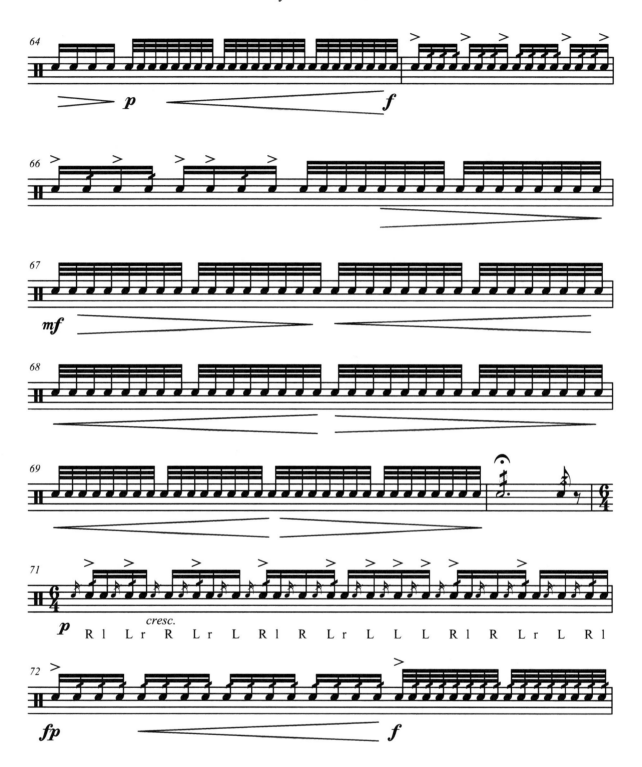

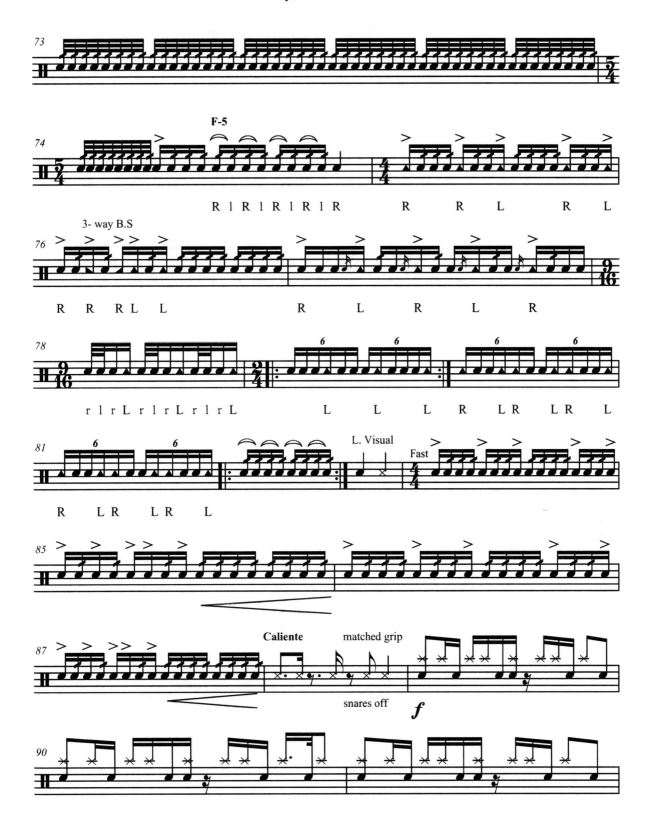

Eye of the Storm

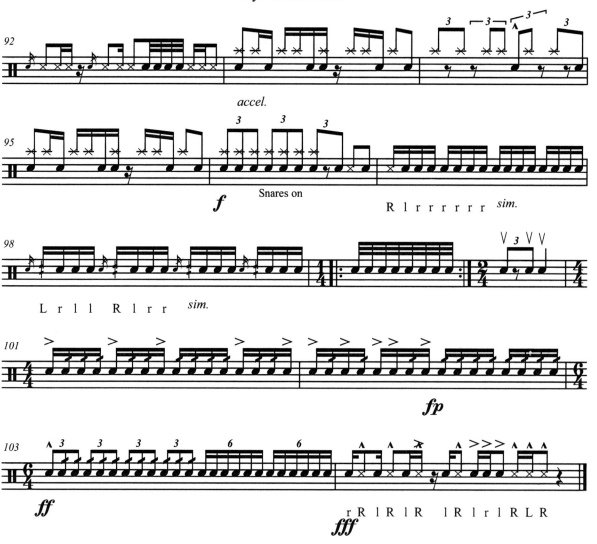

Money $hot

PASIC 2003

G. Jackson

134

Money $hot

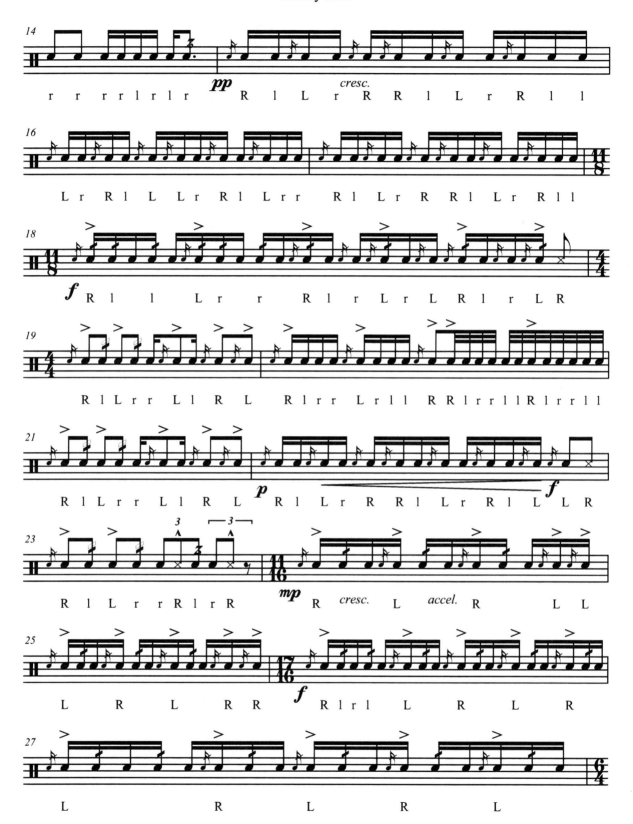

135

Money $hot

Money $hot

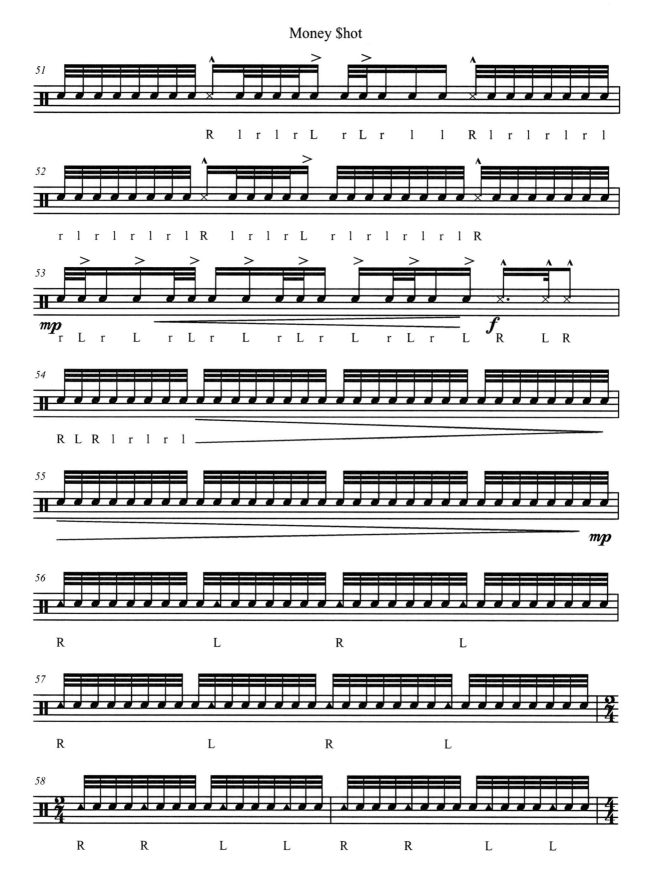

137

Money $hot

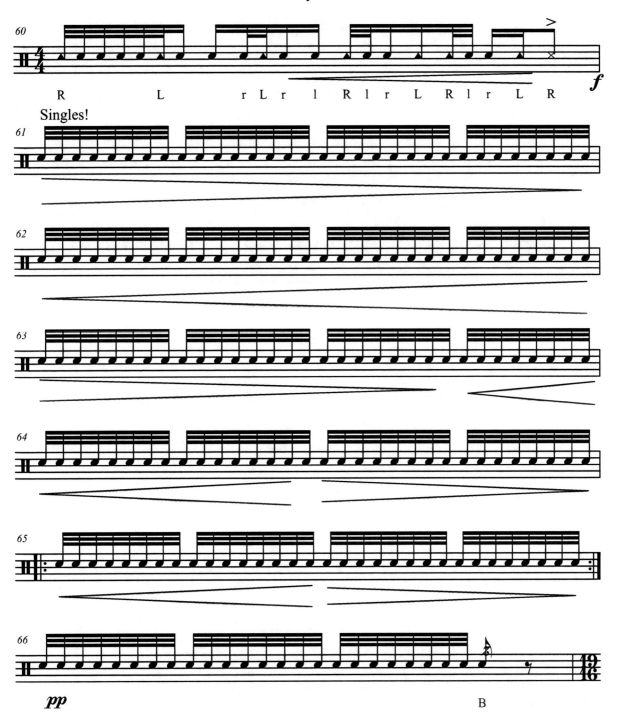

138

Money $hot

Money $hot

Money $hot

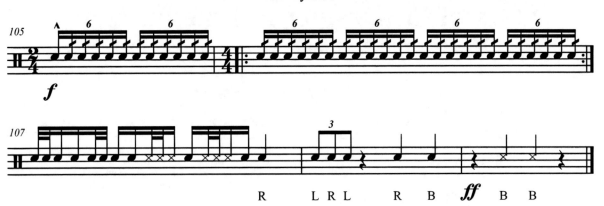

R   L R L   R   B   **ff**   B   B

Story of the Dragon and the Butterfly

PASIC 2004

G. Jackson

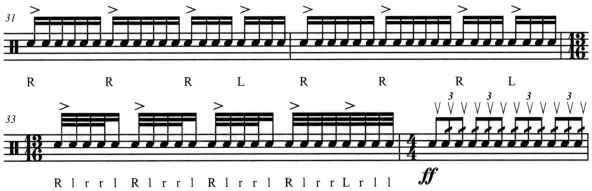

Story of the Dragon and the Butterfly

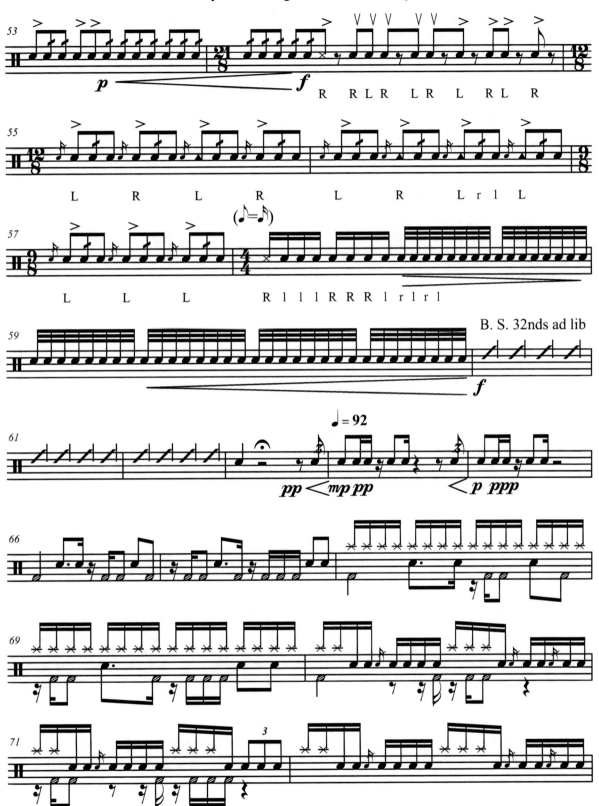

Story of the Dragon and the Butterfly

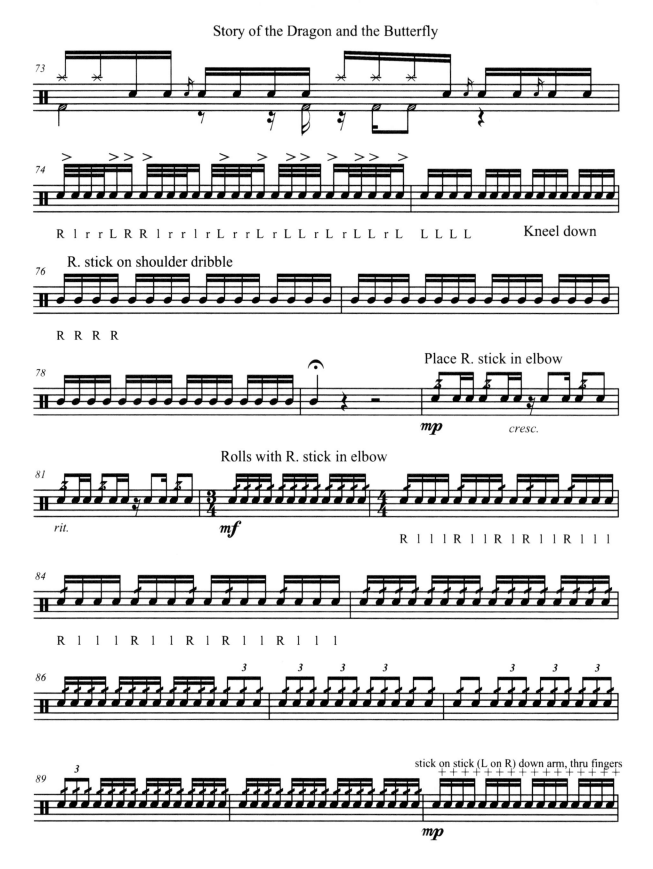

Story of the Dragon and the Butterfly

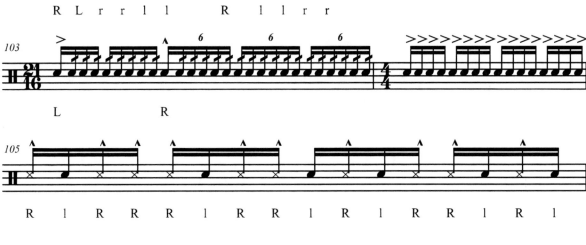

148

Story of the Dragon and the Butterfly

The Elements: Fire and Ice

PASIC 2005

G. Jackson

150

The Elements: Fire and Ice

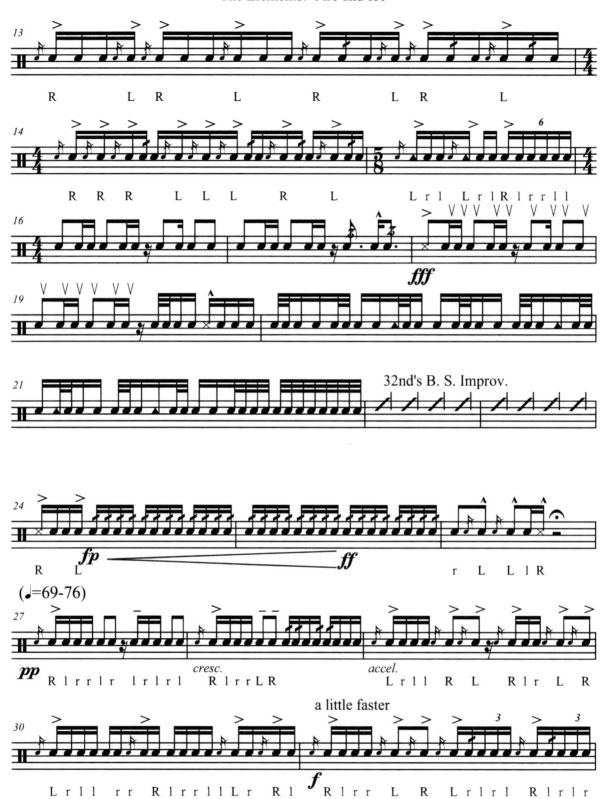

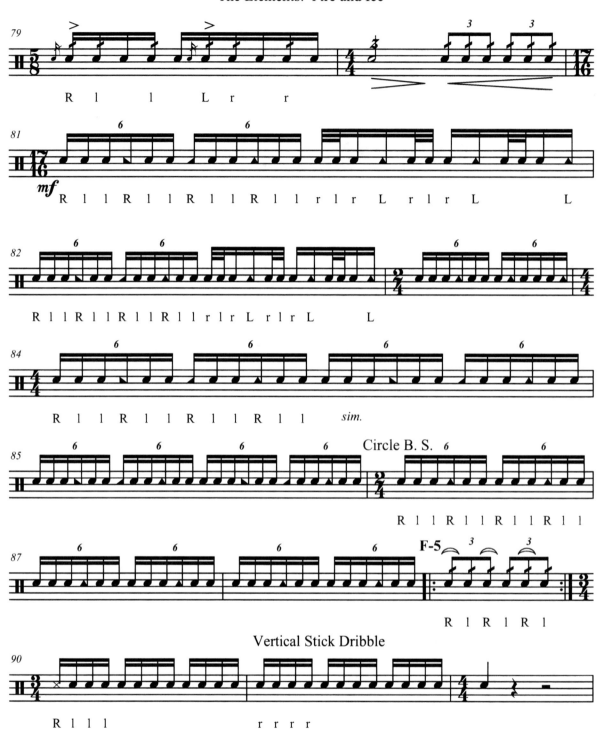

The Excellence of Execution

Part I

G. Jackson

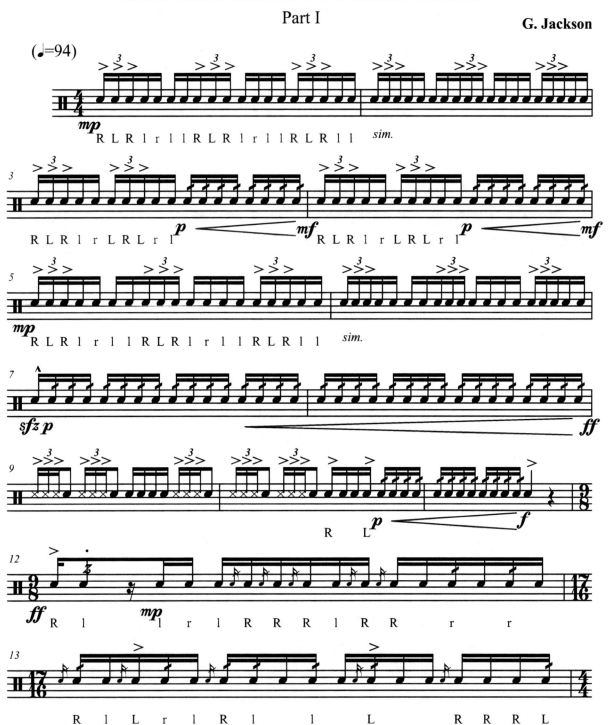

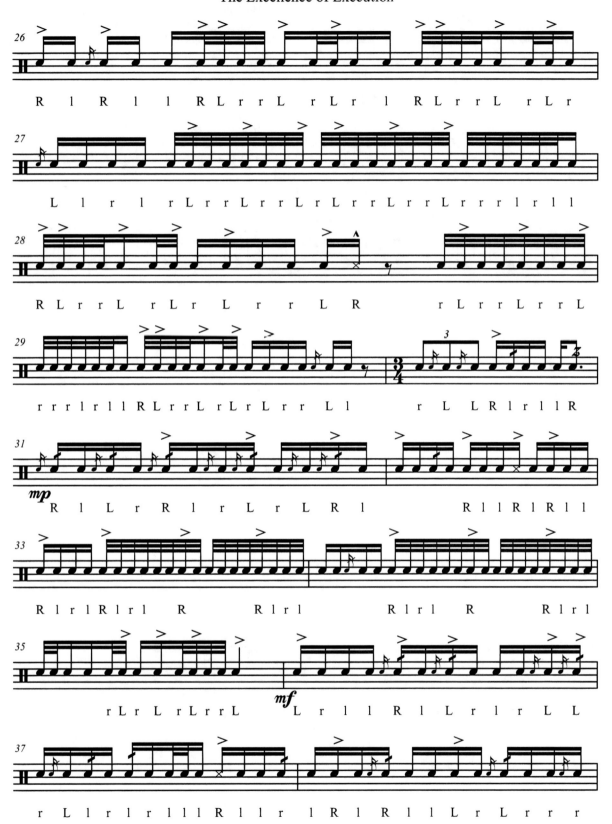

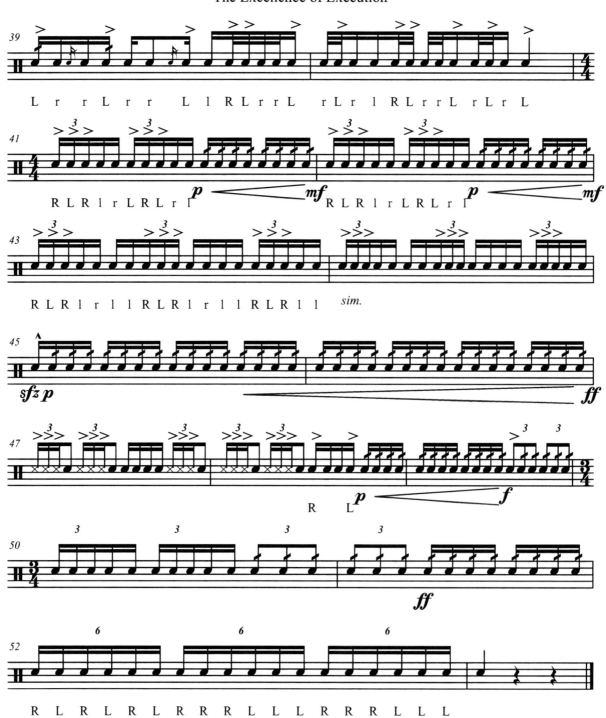

Phenom

Part II

G. Jackson

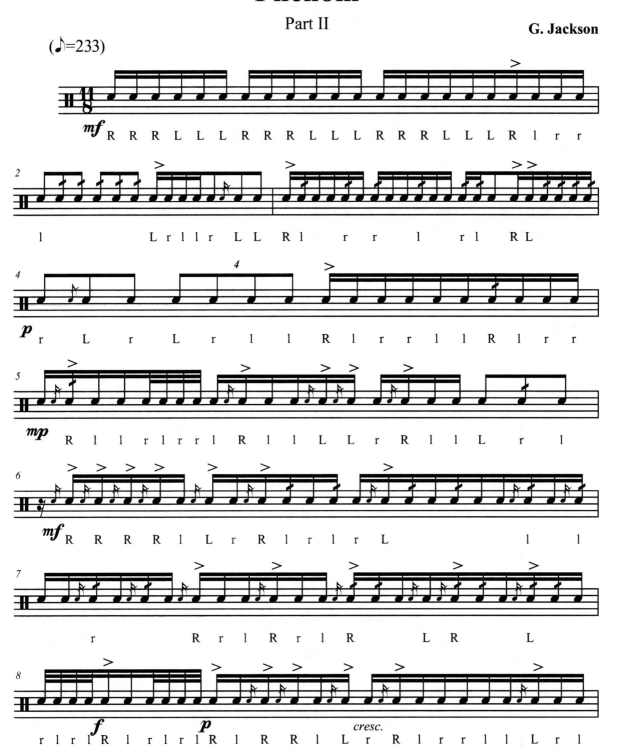

Phenom

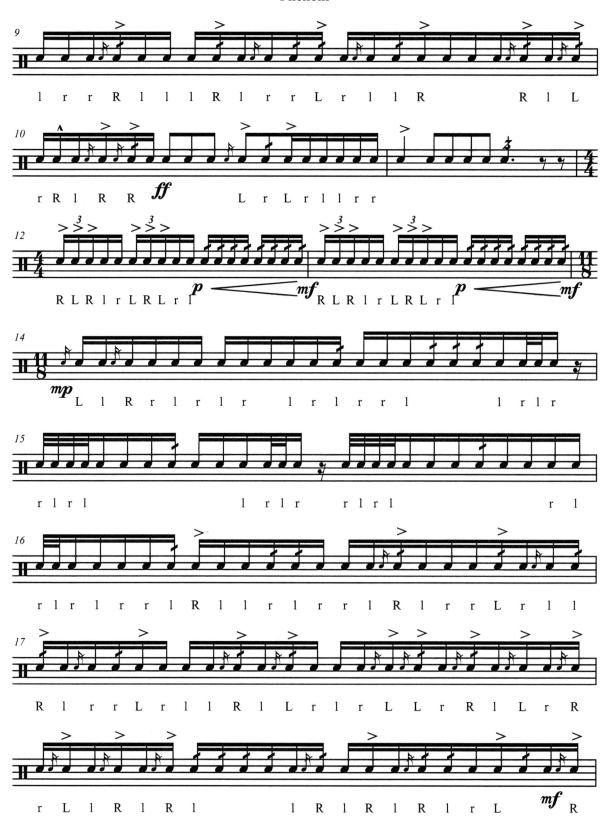

165

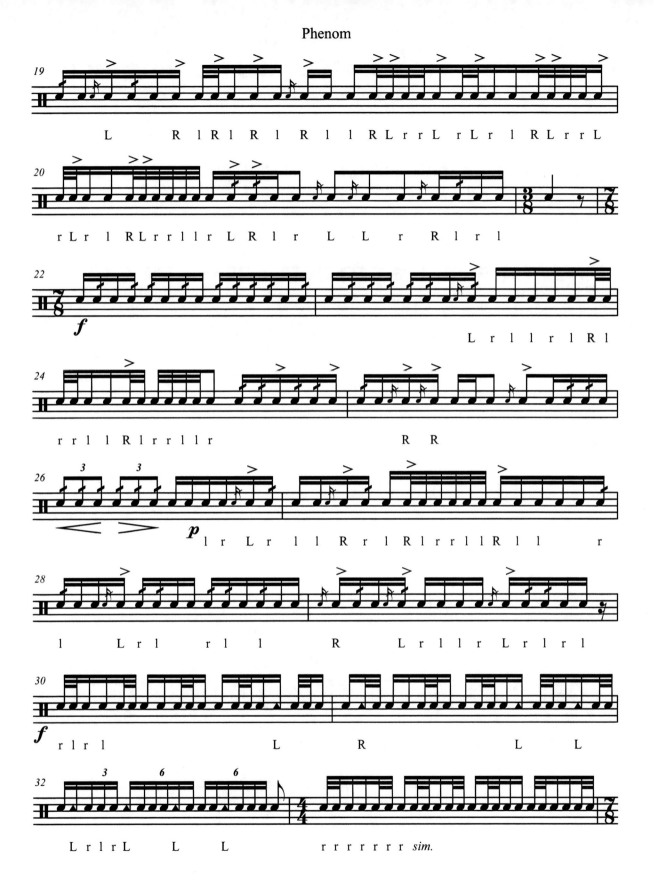

Phenom

Phenom

168

Phenom

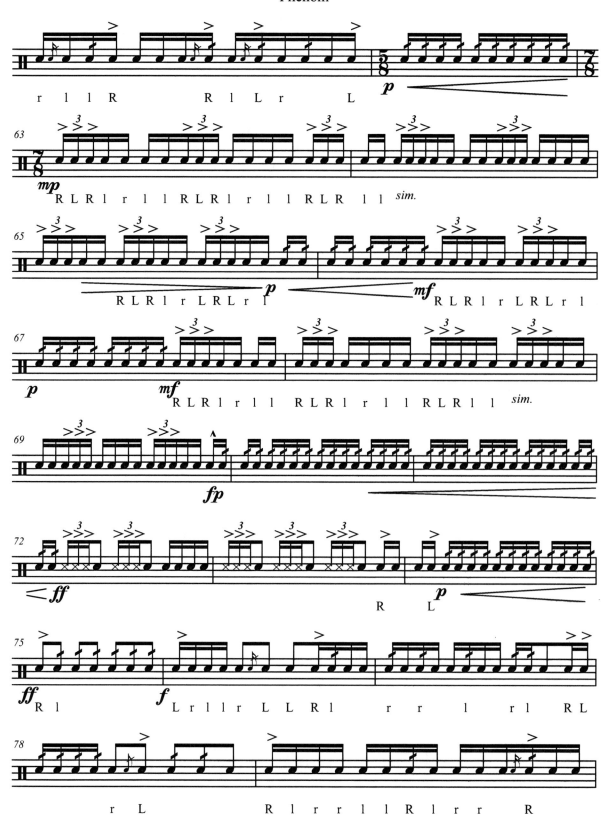

169

Phenom

CPSIA information can be obtained at www.ICGtesting.com
Printed in the USA
LVOW09s1423080515

437343LV00029B/18/P